ONE CHILD AT A TIME

The Mission of a Court Appointed
Special Advocate (CASA)

ONE CHILD AT A TIME

The Mission of a Court Appointed
Special Advocate (CASA)

Yolanda Bryant

CASA
Court Appointed Special Advocates
FOR CHILDREN

ONE CHILD AT A TIME

The Mission of a Court Appointed Special Advocate (CASA)

Copyright © 2014 by Yolanda Bryant

ISBN-10: 0991355075

ISBN-13: 978-0-9913550-7-5

Freeze Time Media

Cover illustration by Di Freeze; cover photos courtesy of CASA

This book is dedicated to my husband, Michael, who overcame an unfortunate childhood; to our four daughters, Rhonda, Natalie, Laura, and Leisha, who taught us the joy of family; and to all of the CASA children for whom I have had the honor of advocating.

Acknowledgments

To share a piece of one's self, while reaching out to help the children around us, is an incredible journey of love, tears, joy, and, above all, hope. I could not be on this journey, nor have written this book without a number of key people. First, I thank my husband, Michael, for his undying love and support, and his endless help with my computer questions. I also thank my daughters, Rhonda, Natalie, Laura, and Leisha for bringing me so much joy in my life, and for being my best cheering squad.

I thank Kelly Hewson and her family for allowing me to share their beautiful journey to becoming a forever family. If I could name the twenty CASA children I have advocated for, I would, but privacy prevents me from doing that. I want each of them to know how much I have cared for them, and how each one of them will always have a place in my heart.

I would not be as well trained or dedicated as a CASA volunteer without the staff at Advocates for Children. I have never worked with a happier, more dedicated group of people than those at the CASA office. I must give a big thank you to the seventeen CASA volunteers that contributed their stories and feelings about being a volunteer. I have been touched and uplifted in hearing each one's experiences. I am also thankful for the legal people that took time from their busy schedules to send comments about CASAs with which they worked.

A book is never complete without the talent of a good editor. I thank my friend Wendy Demandante for her corrections to my first draft. She has an eagle eye. Lastly, the entire book became a reality, pictures and all, thanks to my new editor extraordinaire, Di Freeze. Our minds seemed tuned to the same channel, and because of this, we have a book that pays a beautiful tribute to the unselfish service and dedication of our CASA volunteers.

Contents

Preface   xi

Introduction   xiii

One Child at a Time   1

Addendum to Kelly's Story   51

The Many Faces of CASA   65

What Others Have To Say   105

Preface

In 1977, a troubled judge, David Soukup, looked out over his courtroom filled with adults unable to care for their children and wondered, "Who is for the child?" That year was the first year the number of children in foster care topped just over half a million. Groups of innovative and dedicated citizens, business people, and visionaries assembled. Slowly, CASA — Court Appointed Special Advocates — a movement that brings the community together to advocate for the lives of abused and neglected children, was born.

As the mother of six children, my life was blessed with laughter and love and the knowledge that my children would grow up in a loving, supportive home. However, when I looked around, I found that some of my kids' friends and the children in my kids' schools, in our church, and in our neighborhood were not as happy. The stories of child abuse and neglect would wear heavy on my heart. I joined an organization called the Junior League of Denver and selected CASA as my provisional year placement. My life has never been the same since my first CASA meeting.

My six brothers and sisters, their spouses, my six children and eighteen grandchildren, and my entire extended family have embraced the children in our world who, through no fault of their own, have struggled to find the care, love, family, and security all humans are entitled to feel.

CASA volunteers are your neighbors, friends, strangers, teachers, legislators, and the most generous, giving people I have ever known. They may have little or lots of money. They may have executive jobs or be the stay-at-home parent. They may be a past CASA kid themselves, men and women, young and old, who have heard about the CASA program and, one by one, changed the lives of children.

After thirty years of working as a CASA volunteer, I have established friendships with so many people who want to make a difference and want to work with kids. I often ask our volunteers, "What brought you to our organization?" and the answer is never the same. What is the same is the dedication to see a problem and want to be the solution. CASA volunteers are asked to give an average of eighteen months to the life of a child who has been abused or neglected. Yet I see so many of these CASA volunteers become the lifeline, the constant and lifelong friend to a child. A child who at first reluctantly accepted them and trusted them. In time, the child they would watch graduate from high school, and the child who's children now call them grandparent.

CASA volunteers do not begin knowing that their place in a child's heart will be the reason the child succeeds. They listen to horrific stories, dry tears, scold for bad grades, teach manners, teach tolerance, insist on sibling visits, hold birthday parties, go to court, and make sure that all of the professionals hear the child's voice and know the child's fears and successes. The CASA volunteer teaches the child how to cross the monkey bars and write their names. The CASA volunteer makes up funny stories, and in the end, the CASA volunteer is happy and fulfilled, and the child smiles....

Peggy Rudden,
Executive Director, Advocates For Children, CASA

Introduction

My name is Yolanda Bryant. I have been a CASA volunteer for eight years. I have had several friends ask me about what it is I do exactly. When I explained my work, some of my friends showed interest. I loaned a book written by a previous CASA to one friend that wanted to know more. I thought this would make her excited to help the children. Instead, it scared her away. The tone of the book made her feel that she would have to be a "super hero" to do this kind of volunteer work.

Then and there I decided that some regular person, a grandmother even, needed to write about her experiences and show that the main ingredient needed for this work was love of children. I decided to write about the experiences of an assortment of volunteers. To conclude the book, I included some comments by caseworkers and lawyers that work with CASAs on a day-to-day basis. I enjoyed hearing the stories from the other volunteers and realizing once again the impact one person can have on the life of a child.

My main goal in sharing these stories is to inspire others to join CASA as volunteers. I believe so strongly in this organization that I decided to donate proceeds from this book to my local CASA program.

One Child at a Time

Kelly's Story

April 2007

She was only three years old. I got a call about her as I was driving through the Rocky Mountains toward Utah.

"Yolanda, we have an urgent need situation. Little Kelly has been crying constantly since she was taken from her parents. Do you think you can help us with this case?"

"Yes, I'd love to. I'll be returning home in four days. I'll see her as soon as I get back."

Bright and early Monday morning, armed with my Yahoo map, I headed to the foster home to meet Kelly. I knocked on the door of a two-story house in a middle-income neighborhood. The new subdivision near the airport had few mature trees or bushes. It reminded me of the wide-open wheat fields of Kansas. I much preferred the pine trees and mountain foliage in the neighborhoods closer to the mountains. The front yard had some grass, but it was brown and spotty in several areas. A circular water head was connected to a hose and making a valiant effort to provide moisture to one small corner of the lawn.

As I waited for someone to answer my knock, I noticed the two panels of glass on each side of the door were filled in with some dark material. I wondered why someone would choose to keep light out of her home. Before I could ponder this question further, the door opened and a pleasant-looking black woman smiled out at me. She appeared to be in her late fifties or early sixties. Her hair was cut short and she wore small, dark glasses. She was about five feet, six inches. I could guess this, as we stood about the same height.

As I was processing who this foster parent was, I am sure she was looking at me with the same questioning eyes. At forty-seven years old, I described myself as "everyone's next door neighbor." With shoulder-length, light brown hair; green eyes; a few extra pounds; and a big smile, I had that kind of face that people were drawn to. If a stranger needed directions, they were sure to ask me.

"Are you Alberta Burns?"

"Yes, that's me."

"I'm Yolanda Bryant. We spoke on the phone yesterday. I'm the CASA volunteer for Kelly Dumas. Here is a copy of my court order."

"Come in. Kelly is ready to meet you."

As I stepped inside the semi-darkened front room, I was glad to see other light filtering in from windows in the back of the house. Four young children surrounded me, looking up with curiosity in their eyes, but no one said a word until Alberta gave the go-ahead.

"You children go and get your coloring books. Ms. Bryant is here to see Kelly."

"Okay, Ms. Alberta," said one boy that looked to be about four or five years old. His brown skin and brown hair reflected a Hispanic heritage. His brown eyes twinkled as he grinned at me and ran to get his coloring book.

Two petite, young, black girls turned slowly and left the room. The blank expressions on their faces made me wonder what they were thinking. Lastly, my new charge walked slowly toward me.

"Hi. I'm Kelly," she shyly said.

I looked into her big, blue eyes and saw a confused but curious child. She was tall for her age. Her blonde hair and blue eyes were a stark contrast to the other children in the home.

After greeting me, Kelly turned and ran quickly to get her coloring book, which gave me a couple of minutes to talk with Alberta.

"I don't know if you're aware of what we do as CASA volunteers. The little pamphlet I gave you with the copy of my court order explains our responsibilities in more detail. Basically, the court has asked me to see Kelly at least once a week. I'll visit here today, but normally I'll take Kelly out for at least a couple of hours, if not longer, depending on the activity I plan for each visit. I'll try and work around your schedule as well, Alberta, as I know you have many appointments to juggle since you have four foster children."

"You got that right. Some days we are going to the dentist, some days to the doctor. Some days we have eye checkups. Then every week we have different visits set up through Social Services for each of these kids to see their moms or dads. I used to own my own daycare, so I know how to be organized, but some days there are too many appointments, even for me! That is why I have my twenty-three-year-old daughter, Tanisha, helping with these kids."

"Tanisha, come meet Ms. Bryant," Alberta called toward the kitchen.

A young woman, slightly overweight and wearing an apron over her jeans and T-shirt, popped her head into the living room and said a quick, "Hello, ma'am."

I smiled and gave Tanisha a quick wave before she darted back to whatever she was creating in the kitchen. Just as I turned to resume my conversation with Alberta, four faces appeared around the corner, each carrying a coloring book. The oldest child had a box of crayons. Alberta made the introductions.

3

"This big sister is Sheena. She's seven years old."

Sheena stared at me with cold, dark eyes, without saying a word.

"Her sister is Misha. She's five years old."

Misha smiled and bobbed her head slightly.

"Ramon is our only boy. He's four years old. And you've already met Kelly."

The four children kneeled around a coffee table and began coloring. I positioned myself on the floor between Kelly and Ramon and pulled out a coloring book of my own from the little bag I always brought with me when going on a CASA visit. That day my supplies included several coloring books, crayons, colored pencils, blank paper and pencils, a rubber Gumby and Pokey, and several books geared to a preschooler's interest.

It was quickly apparent that Ramon loved attention. He chattered nonstop and wanted to show me each page he was coloring. I determined after about ten minutes of this activity that I'd need a new plan if I were to have some time alone with Kelly. My supervisor told me that she continued to cry, especially at night, and I wanted her to know as soon as possible that I was her new friend and would be around as long as she needed me.

"Alberta, I think that Kelly and I will go for a walk around the neighborhood."

"Would you like to do that, Kelly?" I asked gently.

"Yes," Kelly replied and then shut her coloring book, jumped up, and gave Alberta a hug. "I'll be back, Ms. Alberta. I love you."

I was surprised at Kelly's declaration of love. Was it normal to have formed such an attachment within only a few short weeks? I was to be surprised again as Kelly and I left the house and began to visit.

As we walked, I talked about what we were seeing around

us — the birds, the houses, the rabbits. I wanted to put Kelly at ease. She quickly joined the conversation, and I found she had a rather extensive vocabulary.

"Do you like bunny rabbits?"

"Yes. They are fluffy and run fast. Do you know where my mommy and daddy are?"

"I don't, Kelly. I'm sorry."

"The people came and took me away from my mommy and daddy. I was crying and crying. I had to go and see a doctor. The doctor gave me a stuffed animal to make me feel better, but it didn't help."

Kelly's words floored me. This three-year-old seemed to have a better understanding of her feelings than many children much older. My heart went out to her.

"I know you miss your parents. The people that took you away are going to set up visits so you can see them."

"I want to see them soon."

"I know you do. I'll try and help make that happen. I'll also visit you every week, Kelly. I was thinking that next time I come we would take a picnic, and go to the park. Would you like that?"

"Oh, yes! Can we go on some swings?"

"You bet. I'll make sure the park has swings."

Kelly and I spent the next few minutes talking about parks and what we liked to do there. Before I knew it, it was time to return to Alberta's and say good-bye for the day. A part of me wanted to scoop Kelly in my arms and take her home with me. With just this short visit, trust had been established, and I knew this beautiful child would look to me for support and guidance. As I drove home that day, I reviewed in my mind how I got started with CASA.

YOLANDA BRYANT

August 2006

My daughter and I pulled up to the freshman dorms in our 1998 Plymouth Grand Voyager. The vehicle was packed to the ceiling with all the necessary boxes and suitcases that an eighteen-year-old is certain she will need for her life away from home.

"Mom, you can pull in here. I want to be close to the main door for unpacking."

Leisha was my last child to leave home. With her long, blondish-brownish hair and bright blue eyes, she was a pretty girl with a winning smile. She had somehow managed to keep her last place in the sibling lineup from instilling the idea of being the baby in the family. Leisha was a capable young woman, eager to be out and exploring life.

After helping her unpack, and giving her a final farewell-for-now hug, I turned the van around and slowly drove out of the dorm parking lot. The thought went through my mind, "Wow, all my children are gone now. I can't believe how fast time has gone by."

As if to reinforce that feeling, the radio in the car began to play, "Then They Do" by Trace Adkins. That was the first time I'd ever heard those lyrics. When he sang, "Now the youngest is starting college," I became teary-eyed with the thought of returning to an empty house after years of parenting four busy daughters.

As I made the eight-hour drive home, I had time to think about the next step in my life. Out of the blue, I remembered a phone call I received from my mother about seven years earlier.

Mom had returned to her home state of Texas, and although she hadn't lived there for almost twenty years, her original accent was creeping into her conversation.

"Yolanda, how are y'all doing?" she asked, her voice full

of excitement.

"Fine, Mom. The kids just started back to school, and it's nice to have some peace and quiet around the house. How are you doing?"

"Great. I want ya to try and guess what I've been up to."

My mind was a perfect blank as I said, "I have no idea, Mom."

"I've been training to be a child advocate with CASA, and I just love this program. Have you ever heard of it?"

"No, I haven't. What's it about?"

"Well, CASA stands for Court Appointed Special Advocate. We work with children that are separated from their families due to abuse or neglect. When Social Services makes them a ward of the court, they assign a CASA to represent the child or children."

"Gosh, that sounds really cool."

Mom spent the next twenty minutes telling me all about her training and how excited she was to help children in this way. I agreed with her that it seemed like a wonderful organization.

My mother moved from Texas shortly after finishing her CASA training and never actually participated in the program. Little did I know that this one conversation back in 1999 would stick with me and surface again just as I was dropping off my last child at college. I thought about that conversation over the next few weeks — especially when I'd wander through my empty house and think, "I sure enjoy the peace and quiet, but I miss the daily interaction with my children and their friends."

The following month, September, I was skimming through our local paper when a small, corner ad caught my eye. The ad was only nine lines. However, here was information about the CASA organization, a plea for volunteers to help in the lives of abused and neglected children, and a phone number and website for more information.

Here was the organization my mom told me about seven years ago! I had not heard anything more about it since our conversation. My mind raced with ideas about this work. I loved children. I had both the time and the desire to reach out to those who were less fortunate. That same day, I dialed the number in the ad and was connected to a pleasant voice.

"This is Advocates for Children. Justine speaking. How may I help you?"

"I saw your ad for an upcoming training and am interested in this volunteer work."

"Great! Let me connect you to Paige. She handles our interviews for new volunteers."

Within a few seconds I was speaking with Paige.

"How did you hear about our organization?"

"My mother trained with CASA in Texas several years ago. She moved suddenly without getting a chance to help any children, but she told me all about your program. I remember thinking that it would be a wonderful organization to volunteer for when my children were grown. My last daughter left for college a few weeks ago. I saw your ad in our local paper this morning."

"Sounds like you already have some information about us. I'd love to meet you and have a short interview. How soon can you come in?

"I can come in tomorrow or Wednesday."

"Wonderful. Our next training starts in two weeks, so we need to interview you as soon as possible. We'll do a background check as well, and that can take some time. How about three p.m. tomorrow?"

"That works for me."

"You have our address, right?"

"Yes, I do. And I'll use a Yahoo map to make sure I don't get lost."

"Sounds good."

As I hung up the phone, I began to feel excited about what this work could entail. Raising four daughters gave me a lot of experience with children and a great love for the welfare of young people.

The next day I found my way from my home to the CASA office. The building was located on a small side street off of a busy main road. The gray building was a perfect box shape, with a set of twelve wide steps on the southeast side, leading to the front door. The bright red CASA emblem decorated the front of the plain building. As I stepped inside, I noticed the office was neat and clean, but furnished sparingly. I would learn in the coming months that this organization was dedicated to using most of their funds to benefit the children directly.

Justine greeted me at the front desk. I recognized her cheerful receptionist voice as the same one that had answered my initial call. Justine put me at ease immediately with her happy greeting.

"Welcome to our CASA office. You must be Yolanda. Paige is expecting you. If you can take this questionnaire into that first room and fill it out, Paige will join you in a few minutes."

After the usual questions such as name, address, education, employment, family names, and "how did you hear about us?" I began to write a little slower as the questions became more pointed and caused me to pause and consider before writing. Some of those questions were:

Have you ever been exposed to an incident of child abuse and neglect?

Not personally.

Have you ever worked with abused or neglected children? Abusive families?

A little bit from my work as a coordinator of a relief organization within my church.

Have you ever been a victim of physical, sexual, or emotional abuse or domestic violence?

Although I haven't had direct experiences in my own life with abuse, I've worked through our church help organizations with several families dealing with these issues. My husband was also a victim of abuse in his childhood, and so I've become very aware of the needs of children living in dysfunctional families.

If you have been a victim of abuse, please discuss how you have handled this/these experience(s), including the length of time spent with a therapist, when that occurred, and whether or not you are presently in therapy.

N/A

Describe your temperament and how you work with others.

Through the years, I've had many opportunities to be in charge of groups. I also have assisted others in leadership positions. I like to say, "I can be a good commander and an equally good follower." My temperament is one of optimism, and I believe in giving people the benefit of the doubt.

When Paige entered, I saw a tall, willowy, young lady, perhaps in her middle twenties. She was dressed stylishly and greeted me warmly with a smile and handshake.

"I see you've finished our lengthy questionnaire."

"Yes. I found the questions very thought-provoking."

"We need to ask probing questions, as this type of volunteer work can be intense and involve many different types of children and families. Our volunteers must have a strong desire to help and to be unafraid of conflict."

"That makes sense."

"You mentioned briefly on the phone how you knew about CASA. Can you tell me a little more about that?"

As I launched into my story about my mother and then finding the little write-up in our local paper, I could see that Paige was listening closely and truly wanted to know what kind of volunteer I might become.

After Paige gave me a brief history of the creation and objectives of CASA, she proceeded to ask me some direct questions.

"What attracted you to CASA?"

"I want to have the chance to help children."

"What aspects of being a CASA volunteer interest you the most?"

I'd thought about this already, so my answer was more detailed.

"The idea that I can become a child's friend and advocate until their life is straightened out sounds like it would be very rewarding. Another less important reason is I am quite interested in learning how the court system works for children and families. There was a time in my younger years when I considered studying law."

"You'll definitely learn much about our court systems as you do this work," Paige continued. "Given that this volunteer opportunity involves children and their sometimes delicate relationships with their families, would you feel comfortable sharing with us a brief description of your childhood and your relationship with your family?"

I launched into a brief history of my childhood.

"I grew up in Southern California with one sister who was three years younger than me. When she was six and a half years old, she got cancer. She died when she was eight. This tragedy tore my parents apart. However, they were determined that their only living child would not be without both parents. Although they did not have much of a marriage after my sister's death, my parents didn't divorce until I was twenty-one. From eleven on, I was an only child. My parents loved and supported me unconditionally. I vowed to one day have a family, hopefully with several children, so that my home would always be full of noise and fun and activity. I didn't care for living in such a quiet home after losing my sister."

"I can see by the questionnaire you filled out that you were able to make that wish come true of having a fun and noisy household. I bet four daughters made for lots of excitement."

"You can say that again!" I chuckled.

Paige was quickly back to business.

"Our cases typically involve one or more of the following six issues. We ask this question of all our volunteers, not to deter or prevent you from working with CASA, but rather to determine which type of case would be the best fit for you.

Paige showed me a list with these six issues and asked, "Could you please tell us a little bit about your level of personal experience with these issues?"

Physical abuse
Sexual abuse
Domestic violence
Alcohol abuse
Drug abuse
Mental illness

"Let's see," I pondered for a moment. "For the first four categories, my only experience is what I've heard from my husband. We have read and reviewed many self-help books, to help both my husband and me learn how to cope with these issues and how to make life what we want it to be, despite his troubled childhood.

"Concerning drug abuse, I have had no previous experience, unless you want to count watching my mother become addicted to Valium as she tried to deal with the loss of her child. And for mental illness, I helped several women from my church group when they suffered with breakdowns."

"I would say you have had some significant experience, Yolanda. Would you feel comfortable taking a case that involved one or more of these issues?"

"Yes, I think I could deal with these problems."

"Another thing to consider is that our cases involve people from all backgrounds and all walks of life. Is there a particular culture, ethnicity, or sexual orientation that you would prefer not to work with?"

"No," I quickly answered.

Paige smiled.

"We just have a few more questions. Have you or a family member ever been involved in a case with the Department of Human Services?"

"My husband was as a child."

"Do you have a particular opinion of DHS?"

"Not really. I don't know much about the Department of Human Services," I answered honestly.

"And that is not a problem, Yolanda. You'll learn all about it during training and as you begin your first case."

Paige's last questions were about my ability to commit to thirty hours of training, and then with a case, if I'd be able to give at least ten hours per month and be able to stay with a case until it closed, which generally took twelve to eighteen months. I replied positively to all of these queries.

After the question-and-answer period was over and I still expressed a strong desire to be a volunteer, Paige discussed with me the guidelines and expectations of being a CASA volunteer. She collected a few needed items from me, such as my driver's license, a copy of my current auto insurance, a check for thirty dollars to offset the background check charges, and a signed statement of commitment. By law, they'd do a background check, and I was told this would take a couple of weeks.

The face-to-face part of the interview went well. Paige was an upbeat interviewer and mainly wanted to understand my reasons for considering this type of volunteer work. I knew I wanted the opportunity to help children have the security and warmth they deserved while trying to deal with family hardships that were in no way their fault or their responsibility. I thought about my husband during the interview. I knew that his young years would've been safer and more stable if he had been assigned a friend and advocate, such as a CASA volunteer.

"I can see that you have the right motivation, Yolanda. We'd love for you to join us for our upcoming training in October. Your background check should be done by then, so you'll be all set to start. How does that sound?"

"That sounds great!"

As I smiled at Paige and prepared to leave, I looked around the small room and saw several bins of toys and books.

Paige seemingly read my mind.

"This is one of the two rooms we use when one of our advocates wants to bring children to a place where they can play and relax. These rooms are used more in the winter, when it may be too cold to go to a park or other outdoor spot."

As Paige gave this explanation, I noticed a play kitchen; a high chair; and some giant, stuffed animals, in addition to the bins I'd noticed at first.

"This area is also used for parents cleared for supervised visits that can be done somewhere other than at the Department of Human Services. This way you, as the volunteer, can bring the family together and be in a safe, controlled environment."

"These rooms seem like a good resource," I commented.

Without any training or experience as a CASA, I wondered to myself how difficult it would be to get a family together for a visit. I'd be finding the answer to this question within a few months. Little did I know then that I would be bringing Kelly here to read books, put together puzzles, and play house.

April 2007

I'd arranged with Alberta to see Kelly three days after our first visit, as I knew she'd been crying daily and had seen no one from her family since arriving at her foster home. As I drove, I replayed in my mind the things I'd learned from Amber, the caseworker, as we exchanged emails the previous week:

"Kelly and her father were found at the Super 8 Motel. Kelly had no clothes on and her hair was full of lice. There was almost no food in the room. After Kelly was examined, it was determined she had not been sexually abused, but she was definitely neglected in the areas of food and clothing. Her father was unemployed. There was a warrant out for her mother's arrest, for a scam she was pulling on senior citizens. She would take Kelly with her to the doors of the elderly and ask for money. Having a child with her made the pleas appear more genuine. The mother has not been found yet."

In hopes that Kelly wouldn't have to stay in foster care long, I emailed the caseworker and the guardian ad litem (GAL) and asked if there were any relatives that might be able to take her. The GAL is the lawyer that represents the child in court. In this case, the GAL I'd be working with was Laura. Both she and Amber were very good about sharing information and quickly responding to my emails. This time Laura replied with the following:

"There is an aunt in town, as well as the maternal grandparents. We have begun background checks on these relatives, but so far it is not looking good. The aunt appears to have some learning disabilities, and grandma and grandpa have criminal records."

I thought of this sweet child without a nearby relative who could be considered safe. I became more determined than ever to not only be Kelly's advocate, but also her friend, whom she could trust at all times.

For this visit, I brought a car seat and a bag with a picnic, some children's stories to read, and some coloring books. If we got tired of the swings, I could read to Kelly or we could color together.

"Hello, Alberta. How are things going with everyone today?"

"Oh, you know, appointments here, appointments there. I gotta take Ramon to the dentist at one. What time did you say you'd bring Kelly back this afternoon?"

"I was planning on bringing her back at three o'clock. Will that work with your schedule?"

"How about three thirty, so I can pick up the girls from school at three ten and be back to meet you?"

"That will be fine. We'll see you here at three thirty."

Kelly was peeking from behind Alberta as this conversation took place. She was dressed in hot pink shorts and a bright pink and yellow T-shirt. Her white sandals looked new. Her hair was wet and appeared a bit sticky.

"I've been working on Kelly's hair every day since she got here," Alberta explained. "They told me down at Social Services to use this particular shampoo and rinse to get rid of the lice. I cut her hair real short too, and I hope that helps. I just finished her rinse, so she'll be wet for a little while. I can't use a blow dryer with this treatment."

Kelly looked up at me with puzzled eyes. She seemed embarrassed by this conversation. I gave her a big smile.

"Are you ready to go to the park, Kelly?"

"Oh, yes!"

Kelly jumped from behind Alberta and grabbed my hand. I marveled at how readily she trusted me.

As we walked hand in hand to the car, I explained to Kelly our plan for the afternoon.

"I packed a picnic for us. I thought we'd go to the park by the reservoir. They have swings and slides there, and maybe even some ducks. How does that sound?"

"That sounds good. I'm getting hungry already."

As I strapped Kelly into her car seat, I asked her what she had eaten for breakfast.

"Oh, I had some juice and cereal. But I'm always hungry."

I thought about the filthy motel room that had served as Kelly's "home." Three meals a day may have been a luxury unknown to her in her first few years of life.

"Would you like to eat some apple slices while we drive to the park?"

"Yes, please," Kelly chortled.

I got out a bag of apple slices and a small bottle of water and arranged them on the sides of Kelly's car seat, which came with a cup holder and an extra section for snacks. This type of car seat would prove invaluable for transporting a variety of CASA children over the next few years.

The drive to the state park took only about twenty minutes. During that time Kelly munched on her apples and we played a simplified version of "I Spy."

"I spy a yellow truck, Kelly. Do you see one?

"Yes, yes, right there!"

"Now I spy a red car. Do you see one?"

Kelly pointed excitedly to a red car near her window. This game got us all the way to the park. Our first activity upon finding a bench under a tree was to eat our lunch. Kelly ate so quickly I thought she might make herself sick. I made a suggestion before the cookies.

"Let's save these for a little later. I think our stomachs need to rest after all that food."

"Okay. Can we go find the swings now?"

We spent a good hour going between the swings and the slides. Kelly smiled and smiled, always ready to go higher and higher when she was on the swings. We took a break to find the ducks. I had saved a few bread pieces to feed them, but Kelly was afraid to get too close, so we watched them from a safe distance. This was her time to feel warm, safe, and secure. If ducks were scary, then we would avoid ducks. Back at our bench we ate our cookies, and I read aloud to Kelly.

That morning, just before I headed to Alberta's, Amber informed me that they had arranged a visit for Kelly to see her grandparents at the Department of Human Services on Friday. Therefore, I was ready with an answer when Kelly asked me an important question.

"Do you know when I get to see my mommy and daddy?"

"I'm not sure when you'll get to see your mommy and daddy, but I do know that tomorrow you'll be going to see your grandma and grandpa. What do you think of that?"

"Yippppeeee! I love my grandma and grandpa. Do you think Mindy will be there too?"

I learned that Kelly's aunt had a child near Kelly's age and that her name was Mindy. I hadn't been told that the aunt would be part of the family visit, but that didn't mean it wouldn't happen. Any relative could visit at the department, since closed-circuit television monitored the visits.

"I think there's a chance that Mindy will be there too."

I hoped my prediction would be correct, as Kelly's face lit up at the thought of seeing not only her grandparents, but also her cousin.

As we left the park that day, I resolved to look into Kelly's lice problem to see if there was anything I could do to help. Kelly told me in the course of the afternoon that when Ms. Alberta washed her hair, the other children called her names, like ugly.

"But you know that's not true, right, Kelly? You are a beautiful, young lady."

"Well, Sheena always tells me, 'You is ugly, Kelly.'"

"That is just not true. You have a beautiful face and beautiful eyes, Kelly. I want you to remember that, okay?"

Kelly looked up with her serious blue eyes, and a tentative smile began to form.

"Okay. I'll try and remember."

I could see it taking some time to undo the mean remarks she was hearing at her foster home. I decided to visit again within a few days, to see if these comments were a onetime thing or a reoccurring problem. I'd also ask how the visit went with Kelly and her grandparents.

We loaded up the car and drove back to Alberta's home. We knocked on the door several times, to no avail.

"I guess Ms. Alberta is late picking up Sheena and Misha from school. We can sit on the porch and talk until they return."

"See that bird?" Kelly pointed and asked. "I think he wants a drink from the sprinkler."

The same circular water head that I saw on my first visit was now set up in a new section of the lawn, trying once again to bring life to the brown patches of grass.

"I bet you're right. That bird is hopping all around the water."

"Do you think he can get a good drink?"

"Maybe, if he opens his mouth really big."

I smiled as I watched Kelly concentrating on the little bird's efforts. We spent about twenty minutes waiting for Alberta and the others. As the children exited the van, I kept a close eye on the oldest, Sheena. I saw her shove Ramon out of the way and yell at her sister, "Hurry up and get out!" As I watched Sheena, my concerns for Kelly increased.

As soon as I got home, I sent a quick email to the case-worker and the GAL:

"I want to let you know that I just got back from visiting with Kelly for the second time. It seems the oldest foster child, Sheena, has been calling Kelly "ugly." This happens when Alberta is doing the daily shampoo routine for Kelly's lice. I know Kelly is crying daily and missing her family. She does not need other children treating her unkindly. I will visit her again in a few days and will let you know if the situation has improved."

19

Both Amber and Laura responded to my email similarly, thanking me for spending extra time with Kelly and asking me to let them know the update on the situation at the foster home.

I asked Alberta whether I could come for Kelly the following Tuesday morning, the day after she was scheduled to see her grandparents. Tuesday couldn't come soon enough for me. This time I barely knocked on the door when a harried-looking Alberta opened it and greeted me.

"Come in, come in. Land's sake, these kids are driving me nuts. Sheena refuses to obey, and I had to call Social Services about her."

I decided I would add my concerns to Alberta's Social Services report.

"You know, Alberta, I was planning on talking to you about Sheena. She's been calling Kelly 'ugly,' and I'm worried she might be saying more than that."

"Well, it wouldn't surprise me. Both Sheena and Misha were abused by their parents, and all Sheena knows how to do is talk mean and use violence to get what she wants. I was hoping I could help these girls by showing discipline and love at the same time, but I'm running out of patience."

"What did Social Services say when you called them?"

"They told me that right now there are no other homes available to take the sisters, and they gave me a couple of suggestions on how to discipline Sheena. I sure hope the ideas work, because I'm growing mighty tired."

"I wish you luck in dealing with Sheena. I'll be keeping a close eye on Kelly and how she's dealing with the other children. I know she had her first visit with her grandparents yesterday. How did that go?"

"Well, I'll tell ya, that was another situation I had to deal with. She was excited to see her grandparents. Her aunt and little cousin were there as well. Kelly jabbered away the whole

NE CHILD AT A TIME

hour, I was told. But when I came to pick her up, that was a different story. She cried and cried and clung to her grand-mother. She didn't want to come back with me."

"That's understandable. How did you finally get her to go with you?"

"The caseworker had to pick up Kelly and carry her to the car for me. She cried most of the way home. And, of course, Sheena just kept telling her, 'shut up, crybaby.' That didn't help anything."

"I'm planning to take Kelly to the county fair today. I thought she'd need some extra attention today; the fair will be a nice distraction for her. We'll return about four o'clock, if that's all right with you."

"Sure. I bet Kelly will enjoy that. Maybe that will help her feel better too."

Alberta called up the stairs for Kelly to come down. Little feet came clattering down the stairs, and there stood a quiet, little girl, her blue eyes fixed steadily on me.

"Hello, Kelly. I'm excited to see you. We're going to a fair. Do you know what that is?"

She shook her head no.

"It's a place with little animals to pet and fun rides. How does that sound?"

"What kind of animals will be there?

"I think there will be some goats and pigs and maybe some small horses."

"Oh, I like those animals."

She quickly took my hand and off we went.

After getting lost for about an hour, we finally found the fairgrounds. All the time in the car, Kelly never complained. We played "I Spy" and talked some more about the different animals we might be seeing at the fair. I brought a couple of hats for us to wear. When we got out of the car and I put my hat on, Kelly giggled.

21

"You look funny."

I laughed with Kelly as I put her hat on her head.

"Well, you look beautiful. Now let's go find those rides and animals."

All afternoon Kelly's eyes were big as saucers as she took in all the sights and sounds that made up the fair. We rode the children's train three times because Kelly was so excited by the colorful cars and the little horn that blew to announce their arrival and departure.

Kelly wasn't afraid of any of the animals, and we spent a good hour petting them in the various pens. She wanted to spend the most time with the baby pigs. Every time they squealed, Kelly would giggle uncontrollably. I dreaded telling her that we would need to go soon.

"We'll have to go in about fifteen minutes," I told her at about three o'clock. "Is there one last ride you would like to go on?"

Kelly looked up sadly, but didn't complain.

"Can we go on the train again?" she asked.

"Of course, and we'll get some cotton candy to eat on the way home. How does that sound?"

The ride home was quiet as Kelly ate her cotton candy and then nodded off to sleep, still clutching her half-eaten bag of sticky, pink confection. I hated to return her to where a bully resided and the foster mother was at her wit's end in dealing with the children. I wondered what I could do to get Kelly out of this situation.

When I dropped off my small charge, I asked Alberta if I could see where Kelly slept. As a CASA volunteer this is something we are asked to do, so that we can include the living conditions in our court report.

Alberta was accommodating. I saw three cribs lined up in a family room, with a television near the beds. I wondered how often the sound of a TV announcer lulled the children to sleep. I presumed Sheena had a bed somewhere else in the house. When I returned home that day, I sent another email to Laura and Amber:

"I took Kelly to the county fair today. She loved riding the train and petting all the baby animals. She would've loved to stay all day. She continues to mention that Sheena calls her names, like 'ugly.' The foster mom, Alberta, seems at a loss in dealing with this angry child. She told me she called Social Services to see whether Sheena and her sister can be moved. However, there are no homes available at this time. I worry about Kelly, as she is so young and is missing her family terribly. She doesn't need to have another child picking on her. I'll try and see Kelly twice a week until I know that she's in a safe environment.

Meanwhile, can you tell me whether you have heard anything from Kelly's parents? I know that they didn't come for the first visit at the Department of Human Services. Is her mother still in jail? Do we have a phone number or another way to reach her father? I'd appreciate any information you may have."

Unfortunately, neither the guardian ad litem nor the caseworker had any new information about the parents' whereabouts. They each thanked me for being vigilant in watching over Kelly.

I called Alberta the next morning and set up a visit with Kelly for that Friday. I decided quiet time at a park would be a nice distraction for her. I looked through my CASA bag and decided to add a few more books, a rubber super ball, and a stuffed bear. I already had enough crayons and coloring books. The little bear was helpful when I wanted to make a child laugh or give them something to squeeze if they were feeling sad. I wasn't sure how Kelly would be feeling when I arrived on Friday.

I also added my camera to the bag. What the judge or magistrate especially enjoyed about our CASA reports, besides our findings, were any pictures we added. The reports that the judge receives from the guardian ad litem and the caseworker are thorough, but those reports don't have pictures. Our reports, with pictures, make the children "real" to the judges.

We can request that the copy of our report for the judge have color pictures. The other copies, which are given to the caseworker, the guardian ad litem, and the child's family, are entirely in black and white. CASA works on a shoestring budget, so black and white copies are needed.

I couldn't wait to take pictures of Kelly, a beautiful child with a warm and happy smile. However, I wouldn't find Kelly smiling on Friday. As I started to buckle her into her car seat, I noticed a bruise on her forehead.

"What happened to your head, Kelly?"

"Sheena pushed me down and called me 'ugly.'"

I was seething inside. The whole purpose of being a volunteer advocate was to make sure children were safe and protected for as long as it took to close their cases. This sweet child had lost her family and was now being abused by another child in her foster home. I wouldn't let this happen again.

I kept my thoughts to myself as we drove to the park. I knew what I needed to do as soon as I returned home, but for now I would spend the next few hours loving this child and helping her forget about her worries, pains, and fears.

"Kelly, that was very wrong of Sheena to push you down. I'm going to talk to Ms. Alberta and make sure this never happens again, OK?"

"I want my mommy and daddy," Kelly said, looking at me with tear-filled eyes.

"I know you do, honey, and I wish I could find them for you. I do know you have another visit with your grandmother and grandfather in a few days."

Kelly brushed back her tears as she managed a small smile,

threw her arms around my neck, and thanked me.

Where did this child learn to be so loving and patient? Her wisdom was beyond her three years. One more idea crossed my mind. It appeared Kelly received love and care during her short life, whether it was from her own parents or her grandparents. Her actions, especially when compared to the poor child that was picking on her, spoke volumes. Meanness, as well as love, is learned through life's experiences.

Today Kelly would receive nothing but love and caring from me. We began our "I Spy" game as we drove to a park that was new to us. I tried to give Kelly a variety of activities so that she'd be busy experiencing new things, leaving her little time to think of her family that she missed so much, or the abuse at her foster home.

I researched facts about lice and bought a special comb to use on Kelly's hair. Since the problem wasn't completely cleared up yet, I decided to add that comb to my bag of books and toys. It was still in its package, and I would put it in a special, closed container after using it on her hair. I didn't mention that activity until we spent plenty of time playing, reading and coloring. It was a beautiful day at the park, with the temperature a comfortable seventy-two degrees. We took our bag of supplies and our picnic and left our sweaters in the car.

As I pushed Kelly on the swings, I saw that happy smile slowly make its way back to her face.

"Can I go higher?"

"You bet. Hang on; here we go!"

I pushed her as high as I could. Kelly giggled and squealed and my heart swelled to see her as happy and carefree as every three-year-old child should be.

While we ate our lunch on a picnic bench, I read Dr. Seuss's "Green Eggs and Ham." Kelly looked at the pictures and asked, "Do you like green eggs?"

"I believe I do. I made them once for my four daughters,

and I ate them too. My girls thought it was very funny that we had green eggs and Spam for breakfast."

"What is Spam?"

"It is kind of like ham, but smaller."

Kelly wrinkled her brow as she thought about this.

"Maybe one day I could eat green eggs and Spam."

"I bet you'll be able to."

I sent a quiet prayer to God that this sweet child would soon have a loving family of her own.

As soon as I was home from my visit with Kelly, I sent a quick, urgent message by email to the caseworker and the guardian ad litem. I planned to call them as well, but I wanted my information to be in writing for the record:

"Something must be done immediately to remove Kelly from her present foster home. Not only has the name-calling continued, but also today when I went to pick up Kelly for an outing, she had a large bruise on her forehead. She told me, "Sheena pushed me down." Kelly is suffering enough right now without having to endure abuse on top of everything else. Please let me know how I can help to get Kelly a new placement."

I then left voice messages on both Amber's and Laura's cell phones. Laura was the first to return my call, and she was outraged at what was happening.

"Yolanda, I feel very strongly that this case is going in the direction of termination of parental rights. If this does happen, Kelly will be available for adoption. I think we should look into getting her placed in a legal risk foster home as soon as possible."

"How does a legal risk foster home differ from a regular foster home?"

"Legal risk means that the families are fostering for the main objective of adopting a child when the situation presents itself and the child seems to be a good fit for the family. The 'risk' part of the title implies that until the case is closed there is always the risk that a family will not be able to adopt a certain child, as their parents have at least a year to comply with court orders and thereby have their child/children returned home."

"A legal risk foster home sounds like a great idea for Kelly. Any family would be blessed with this child in their home. How long will it take to complete the process?"

"I'll begin looking through the legal risk foster homes available and set up several appointments to visit the families this week. If we find a viable home, we'll make the transition as early as the beginning of next week. Would you like to go with Amber and me when we make these visits?"

"Yes, I'd love to join you. Just let me know the time and place, and I'll be there."

Amber concurred with all of Laura's ideas. I was glad to know that two hardworking, dedicated professionals were working on Kelly's behalf. I could hardly wait to visit the families that might provide a permanent home for Kelly.

I soon met Amber and Laura at the first house. The neighborhood was nice, and the outside of the home was well kept. As we knocked on the door, I wondered what we'd find on the inside. I wasn't prepared for who met us. My attention went directly to the dog I saw. This animal, the size of a small horse, looked up with big, brown eyes and waited patiently for his master to give a command.

"Please, please, come in. Merlin won't hurt you. He is a big, lovable baby. I'm Olivia."

The woman extended her hand in greeting.

As I looked into Olivia's eyes, I almost caught my breath. The similarities in her face and little Kelly's were remarkable. Olivia's blue eyes, round face, and high cheekbones were just like Kelly's. Even her fair skin was the same shade. Her smile was infectious and spread from ear to ear. I saw them as mother and child without even thinking twice. We walked further into the home and met Jim, Olivia's husband.

"Hallo. I'm very happy to meet you."

Jim's British accent was unmistakable. He was of average height, with a lean build and a partially bald head. He too had a pleasant face, with large, expressive eyes and a smile to match his wife's. Both he and Olivia continued to smile as they led us to a set of couches and introduced us to yet another large dog, a Great Dane named Abba.

"Wow, these dogs are gigantic!" I couldn't help but interject.

"You'd be surprised how gentle they are," Jim explained. "We take them regularly to make rounds at the nearby hospitals. Patients are quite taken with them, actually."

Olivia led Merlin over to me and the two other visitors so that we could pet him and see for ourselves how gentle he was. I was thinking about Kelly and whether she would like these dogs or would be afraid of them. I guessed that since they were well-behaved enough to visit hospital patients they'd surely know how to act with a three-year-old child.

"Merlin and Abba love little children as well as adults," Olivia said, as if reading my mind. "They're trained to be gentle and obedient."

"That's good to know," I commented in a relieved tone of voice.

Amber began the interview by explaining what responsibilities each of us had in relation to Kelly. She gave me a few minutes to explain my role as a court appointed advocate, and then she outlined her job as Kelly's Social Services case worker. Laura then explained that she was Kelly's court appointed lawyer, known as a guardian ad litem. Then, for about five minutes, Amber briefly talked about who Kelly was, why she was taken from her family, and why both Amber and Laura felt that this child was likely to be a candidate for adoption. Jim and Olivia listened with rapt attention.

At this point, Laura switched gears and began asking questions that would help us get a feel for both Jim and Olivia and understand more about their family dynamics. We learned more about Merlin and Abba's trips to visit patients at local hospitals. We learned about Jim and Olivia's jobs. We heard about hobbies, travels, and extended family.

I knew Social Services inspected and approved the home, as that was a requirement before being listed as a possible legal risk home. Olivia, however, was excited to show us the room she'd prepared in the event that one day a child would occupy it.

As we tentatively moved toward the stairway, Merlin, the larger of the dogs, accompanied our every move. We were still not quite sure of his reported gentleness and good nature with people.

"Merlin, sit! Stay," Jim commanded, quietly but firmly. The dog immediately responded and took up a spot at the side of the stairway.

We could see that the report on Merlin was indeed true. These dogs were well trained. We three visitors breathed easier after watching the dog lie down. My dog at home was a third the size of these fellows, and Laura and Amber must have had small dogs or no dogs at all, as they appeared as unsure as I was around these gentle giants.

As we proceeded upstairs, we peeked in a bedroom and a bathroom as we passed by them. Each of these was nicely decorated and clean in every way. The room we were shown for a potential new member of the family was a child's dream. There was a modern bunk bed with brightly colored quilts and stuffed animals. Cubbyholes, each holding a book or toy, covered one wall.

Two child-sized chairs were pulled up to a small table where coloring or Play-Doh activities could take place. The closet was designed to have low hangar rods on the bottom half, so that even a young child could reach at least half of what was hung in the closet. The large window in the room overlooked a lush, green backyard, with a distant view of the mountains complementing the scenery.

As we finished the tour of the entire house, I whispered to Laura, "Would it be okay if I showed Jim and Olivia some pictures of Kelly?"

With Laura's permission, I quickly pulled four pictures from my folder.

"Olivia, I want to show you and Jim a few pictures of Kelly."

I could see the look of joy and happiness on the faces of both prospective parents.

"Isn't she beautiful!" they exclaimed, almost in unison.

As we gathered up our things in preparation to leave, I thought, "I'm ready to bring Kelly here tomorrow!" I knew, however, that two more families deserved to be reviewed as possible candidates.

Before driving away, Amber invited me to visit the other two homes the next day. Unfortunately, I had a previous appointment scheduled and had to decline. I did ask Amber to email me after the visits to let me know how she and Laura were feeling about the three choices.

"I know this is our first visit, but I sure feel good about this family," I offered.

"We'll let you know our assessments of the other two families."

"Thank you. The sooner we get Kelly moved, the better."

By four o'clock the next afternoon, I had emails from both Amber and Laura. Amber wrote:

"For various reasons the last two homes didn't fit with the criteria we are hoping for Kelly. I feel good about going forward with Jim and Olivia. Laura agrees and we are putting in the request for an immediate transfer. We hope to have Kelly moved by Friday."

I was ecstatic! This email came on Wednesday and there was now the chance Kelly could be in this wonderful home by Friday. I sent a silent "Thank you" heavenward.

I emailed Amber and Laura and asked them to tell me when all was ready. I would then visit Kelly and prepare her for this new change. I also asked which of them would advise Alberta of the upcoming plan. Amber said she would call Alberta as soon as the date was official, but that in the meantime I could let her know that this transfer would be happening in a matter of days. I couldn't wait to make that phone call!

"Good morning, Alberta," I said in a calm voice. "This is Yolanda. I just wanted to let you know that a new home has been found for Kelly. Social Services wants to move her by this Friday. Amber will call you as soon as the date is official."

"I'm glad to hear that. I know Kelly will be happier in a different home."

"I'd like to stop by later today and talk to Kelly about this move. What time would be good for me to drop by and take a little walk with her, so we can talk about the new family?"

"Come at three thirty. We should be back from school pickups by then."

"Great. See you then."

As I drove to Alberta's, I thought about the Hewsons and their two giant dogs, their lovely home, and the colorful child's room. I could not wait to introduce Kelly to this possible forever home. One tiny doubt entered my mind.

"Yolanda, this case isn't over yet," I told myself. "By law, Kelly's parents have a year to show the courts they can straighten out their lives and be responsible enough to raise their child."

As I thought about the time that passed since this case first opened, and what I read in the files about Kelly's parents, my gut feeling was that these two people didn't have the desire or the will power to do what the courts asked of them. I did give these parents credit for one thing: because Kelly was such a bright child and she knew how to interact with those around her, it was obvious that she was shown love in some form. Also, it appeared her mother took care of her health, as Kelly did not test positive for any problems that can occur when a mother is smoking, drinking, or doing drugs during pregnancy. For these reasons, I could think about the parents in a positive and kind way. Despite the hardships Kelly went through, this child was lucky enough to have generally good health and the ability to love and be loved.

My thoughts about Kelly were verified when I knocked on the door. As soon as Alberta called for Kelly, she came running down the stairs and straight for me.

"Oh, Ms. Bryant, I'm so happy to see you!" she exclaimed as she threw her arms around me.

This was the first time Kelly used my name since we'd practiced it at the park.

"And I'm so happy to see you, Kelly! I have some fun news for you. Let's take a walk and I'll tell you all about it."

"Is it okay if I go for a walk with Ms. Bryant?" Kelly asked as she turned toward Alberta.

"Of course, child. You go on ahead."

We left the house walking hand in hand.

"Kelly, what would you think of going to a new home where a nice man and lady live?"

"Is that cuz Ms. Alberta doesn't want me anymore?"

"No, it's because this new family is looking for a child to come and live with them, and when they learned about you, they were very excited to meet you."

"Can my mommy and daddy come live with them too?"

"No, your mommy and daddy went somewhere else to live, and we can't find them right now."

"I guess that's why they don't come to visit me?"

"I'm sure they'd come if they could, Kelly, but sometimes parents get in trouble and then they can't visit their children. I'm sorry your parents are having troubles."

"Me too, because I love my mommy and daddy."

"I know. In the meantime, what do you think about meeting Jim and Olivia? They have two really big dogs that are very nice."

"Oh, I love dogs. What are their names?"

"Merlin and Abba, and they're almost as tall as you!"

"I won't be afraid."

We spent the next ten or fifteen minutes talking about the dogs, and about Jim and Olivia. I described the family, the pets, and the house. I wanted Kelly to feel as relaxed and ready to meet the Hewsons as possible.

We were trained in CASA that for first time meetings between children and new placements, it was better to gather in a neutral place. I knew Kelly loved parks and I figured it would be a good place for two big dogs to romp.

"We decided that Jim and Olivia could bring their dogs to that park you and I went to a couple of weeks ago. Remember the park with the swings and the geese? How does that sound?"

"I remember that park. Can you go with me, Ms. Bryant?"

"You bet!"

As things turned out, no one was home the day I went to pick up Kelly from her foster home. Alberta later told me she had too many appointments that day and couldn't get back at the time we had arranged.

Between Laura and Amber it was determined that we would try for a one-day visit at the Hewsons the very next day. Olivia recalled that Thursday:

Laura and Amber came to our house. Kelly walked straight up to Abba, the Great Dane, and gave her a big hug. She walked in like she owned the place. We chatted for a bit and then took Kelly out to the backyard, where we ran with the dogs. We ended up lying on the grass, looking at clouds, and picking out shapes. It was so obvious that Kelly was an articulate and clever girl. She still had a scratch on her face from the other foster child. We gave her a stuffed animal named "puppy Merlin" to take back to Ms.

Alberta's to help her transition. When it was time to go, she cried (but didn't make a fuss) and it broke our hearts, even though we knew she was coming back."

Jim remembers that Kelly was smiling the whole time and was like a pinball in the house, repeatedly asking, "What's that? What's that?"

Since the day visit went so well, the caseworker and the lawyer decided that Kelly could try a full weekend with the Hewsons. If all went well, Amber would go to Alberta's on Monday, pick up all of Kelly's belongings, and officially transfer her to her new, legal risk foster home.

Amber asked if I could bring Kelly for this next step in the transition. I arrived at Alberta's the next morning at nine. Kelly was waiting by the door when I arrived. She looked ready for a visit in her yellow shorts, flowered shirt, and clean white sandals. A small, duffle bag was at her feet.

Before I even said hello, Kelly hopped to my side and blurted out, "I'm ready to go, Ms. Bryant! Will the dogs be there?"

"Good morning, Kelly. Yes, the dogs will be there, along with Jim and Olivia. It looks like your bag is ready; that's great."

"Yes, Ms. Alberta packed it for me after breakfast."

Alberta had been watching our exchange and came to give Kelly a quick hug as we prepared to leave.

"Bye, Ms. Alberta. I love you."

"I love you too, sweetie. Have a good time."

Kelly waved to Alberta as we walked toward the car. Chances were this would be the last time Kelly would see Alberta or the children peering out from behind their foster mother. I said nothing of this possibility to Kelly, as she didn't need to process another set of farewells to a place she was beginning to think of as home. I knew that with the love and affection the Hewsons could give Kelly, this foster home would soon become a vague memory.

Kelly and I chatted about the new place where she'd stay that weekend. The two dogs were always in the forefront of the conversation. Animals had a way of bridging the gap when children needed reassurance or acceptance.

CASA saw this play out each month, as dogs came to the office as part of a program called Wagging Tales. Volunteers can bring school-aged children to the office one Saturday each month. They pick several books and read them to their special dog.

These dogs are trained to sit quietly and watch the child as they "listen" to the story being read to them. Some of the dogs are young and will lick a child as he reads, or put its head in the child's lap. This causes the child to laugh and hug his dog. Then the children continue with their reading. No one corrects the child, and the dog looks as if it is having the time of his life. This makes a child feel good about her reading abilities and loved by her new, furry friend. The first time I took a couple of children to read to the dogs, I wiped away a tear or two, as I watched lonely children connect with playful puppies. The children are never ready for this experience to end.

I remember one little boy saying to me, "I wish I had a dog that would let me read to him." I thought that Merlin and Abba would be the kind of dogs that would help Kelly feel welcomed and loved.

On that sunny, Friday morning, Jim and Olivia, as well as Merlin and Abba, met us at the door. The four of them barely fit in the frame of the doorway.

"Well, hello, Kelly. We've been waiting for you. Please come in."

Kelly's face broke into a big grin and she headed immediately for the Great Dane. She put out her hand to stroke Abba's fur.

"I think he remembers me."

"Would you like to help me feed Abba?" Olivia

asked brightly.

"Oh, yes! I can do that."

I could tell right away that these two people were ready to embrace Kelly with all of their hearts. It appeared that Abba and Merlin were ready for a new friend as well. Just as this new, little family headed to the kitchen where the big dog bowls were kept, there was a knock at the door. Amber and Laura arrived at the same time.

"I'll get the door, Olivia. You all go ahead with the dog feeding."

I wanted a minute in private to tell both the lawyer and caseworker my first impressions of our arrival at the Hewsons.

"Kelly isn't afraid of the dogs at all. Yesterday must have put her completely at ease. She's followed Jim and Olivia right to the kitchen, since Olivia invited her to help feed the dogs. She was delighted!"

"I'm so glad to hear this," Amber joined in. "Both Laura and I feel very good about this home. The final test is how Kelly feels toward the family. This may turn out to be her permanent home."

"I feel that way as well. I'm betting this weekend will be great for not only Kelly, but for Jim and Olivia too."

The three of us hurried to the kitchen to watch the feeding of the pony sized dogs. Kelly giggled as she poured food into a gigantic dog dish.

"Look, Ms. Bryant. Abba is eating my food."

"He sure is. I bet he's glad you came to help feed him."

"Now I'm going to feed Merlin," Kelly explained in an excited voice. "Watch me!"

Olivia handed Kelly another half-gallon container filled with food.

"Merlin's bowl is around the corner. We separate the dogs while they eat, so they don't feel like the other one wants his food."

After all the food was poured and water bowls refilled, we headed to the living room for an opportunity to ask Olivia and Jim some questions. Olivia was completely prepared.

Knowing Kelly would be here, she arranged a small table and chair near the couch and filled it with activities that would catch the attention of any child. Kelly was soon immersed with a drawing board — one that she could draw on with a special pen and then slide a bar to erase everything — ready to start a new picture. While Kelly was occupied, Laura asked Jim and Olivia if they had any specific questions for us about Kelly or this weekend visit. We, in turn, double-checked what their plans were for the next couple of days. We assured them that all three of us were available should any questions or concerns arise.

As the conversation wrapped up, we were all feeling good about this placement. Amber confirmed with Kelly that she would be visiting the home for a couple of days. I squatted down by Amber and watched as this discussion took place.

"Kelly, do you think you'd like to visit here for a couple of days and help Jim and Olivia with their dogs?"

"Oh, yes. I want to stay here for a long time."

Amber and I looked at each other briefly, both amazed at how smoothly this transition was going so far.

"That may be what happens, Kelly. We'll come by on Monday and see how everything is going."

"I'll also call Olivia tomorrow and ask her if you're having a good time," I chimed in. "If you need anything, Kelly, you just ask Jim or Olivia."

"I will, Ms. Bryant. Can I go play with Abba and Merlin? They're done eating and I think they want to play."

"Why don't you go ask Jim if it's okay to play with the dogs?" I guided Kelly to begin the transition.

Kelly looked over at Jim, who was smiling at her from the couch. She hesitated only a few seconds, and then walked resolutely toward him.

"Jim, can I play with your dogs?"

"Of course, Kelly. Do you want to come to the backyard with Merlin and Abba and me? You can help them exercise like you did the other day."

"Oh, yes."

As Kelly followed Jim, we wrapped up the final details with Olivia.

"Here's my card with my cell phone number," Laura told Olivia as she handed the card to her. "If you have any questions, please call."

As CASA volunteers, we too had business cards to give to our families. Amber and I both added our cards to Laura's. I told Olivia that I'd call the next day to see how everything was going. I also told her to call me anytime, as Kelly was my first priority.

I went outside to tell Kelly I was leaving and that I would be back in two days to see how she was doing. Kelly was so busy running with Merlin she barely took time to stop and breathlessly say, "Bye, Ms. Bryant. I'll see you soon."

I left the Hewsons and was ready to burst out singing, I felt so happy and hopeful for my little charge.

I learned later that Jim and Olivia were quite new to this fostering and foster-to-adopt program. Their home was only approved the previous week. They were just finishing their adoptive parent training class when they received an email about a little girl named Kelly that needed a foster-to-adopt home. Their parenting class teacher was happy to hear this news, but warned them that finding a child that fit their family could be daunting, and that it was likely that many applications would come and go before a child was placed with them.

Nonetheless, the Hewsons quickly let the county know that they were genuinely interested in meeting this child.

Olivia later told me, "It was a Wednesday when Amber

called to say that Kelly would indeed be coming to our home. I was visiting a customer and warned them that I was awaiting this very important call and would step out of our meeting when it came. I can remember standing in their break room and receiving the amazing news. I made a quick call to Jim to tell him the news. I finished the call with a rushed request for Jim to meet me after work at Toys"R"Us, so we could get things for Kelly. What followed was a crazy shopping spree the likes of which had never been seen before. We could be heard to exclaim, "I don't know what she likes!" and "That's okay, let's just buy it and we'll find out if she likes it!"

I was anxious to know how Kelly felt after her first overnight at the Hewsons. When I called the next day, Jim answered. He couldn't wait to tell me about Kelly.

"Kelly is such a jewel. She is ever so polite, and just loves playing with Merlin and Abba. Would you like to speak with her, Ms. Bryant?"

"Oh, yes. Thank you, Jim."

Kelly must have been right there with Jim, as right away I heard a cheery, "Hallo, Ms. Bryant!"

I smiled to myself, as I could tell that Kelly had picked up on Jim's British sounding "Hallo."

"Are you enjoying your visit, Kelly?"

"Oh, yes. I want to stay here for a long, long time. Can I, Ms. Bryant?"

Wanting to give hope, but not completely sure of the final outcome, I spoke carefully.

"I think that you should be able to visit for quite a long time, Kelly. How are Merlin and Abba doing?"

Changing the subject to the dogs was just the outlet I needed. Kelly began a long description of her many activities with her newfound, furry friends. We finished our chat with the promise that I would come on Monday to see her beautiful room and play with her dogs and her new toys.

39

After visiting with Kelly, I sent an email to Laura and Amber describing how well Kelly was doing and giving my suggestion that the transition was complete. It was time to see Kelly enjoying every day with this wonderful family. Both Amber and Laura were in total agreement. Arrangements were made and Kelly was legally placed with the Hewsons.

Now the waiting game began. By law, Kelly's parents were given one year from the date the case began in court to prove they were able and willing to care for their daughter. This is determined by how well the parents fulfill the court-ordered stipulations for being responsible parents. Each case is given individual requirements. Some of the most general items are as follows:

1) A parent must show a steady job and paycheck for at least six months.

2) A parent must show the ability to provide adequate housing for their child/children.

3) A parent must go through the proscribed drug rehabilitation as set out by Social Services and provide a document stating they have completed the program.

4) A parent must complete any and all therapy required by Social Services.

5) A parent must complete the required parenting class as described by Social Services.

This list of required items can be daunting if a parent/parents have been in jail, homeless, or are currently battling drug addictions. At times, the love of a parent for a child will give him the strength and determination to beat the odds and bring his family back together. When this happens, there's almost a palpable feeling of joy in the courtroom as the judge takes the time to commend and praise the parents for their herculean efforts to be the kind of parents their child deserves. Other times, you can almost guess the outcome of a case, as month after month a parent doesn't show up for the court review. At times like this you pray for a loving relative or a caring family like the Hewsons.

In Kelly's case, two people in her life continued to show up for family visits. They were her grandmother and her grandfather. At the start of the case, Kelly was always excited to see her grandparents. At times, they brought her aunt and little cousin. As I mentioned earlier, none of these relatives were deemed safe and appropriate adoptive alternatives. As Kelly settled into her life with the Hewsons, these visits became more sporadic. Jim remembered the first time he took Kelly for one of these visits.

"She clung to me the whole time. When it came time to leave, Kelly waved good-bye to her birth family and walked away holding tightly to my hand."

Although I mentioned many of the positive qualities that Kelly possessed, certain obstacles needed to be overcome. Jim and Olivia became intimately aware of these things as time progressed.

The first and most easily solved problem centered around the use of names. Olivia wrote an email to me a couple of weeks into the placement:

"...Kelly is looking forward to seeing you later this week. It would be helpful if you could see if you can use our names a lot and try to get her to use them as well. ... She is struggling with that and we'd like her to feel comfortable with us. She just keeps calling us the man and the lady (although on occasion she does use our names, so we are sure that she knows them)."

I replied to Olivia:

"Thanks for the pictures you sent of Kelly. I will use your names a lot! Don't worry too much about that though; I had the same situation with Kelly. Finally one day, about a month ago, we practiced having her say my name back to me during our entire visit. After that, she was fine. I assume you want me to use your

first names with her? I have her calling me Ms. Bryant, but that's because it's a little more formal, and since I'm not family, that seemed appropriate to me. If there's anything else I can help with, let me know. As the weeks go by, if there's a certain time that you or Jim or the two of you could use a little alone time, let me know. I'd love to watch Kelly."

The most obvious physical problem was the mouth of silver teeth that Kelly displayed. Due to the lack of any dental hygiene her first three years many of her upper and lower front teeth were rotten. The Hewsons knew what to do for that situation, so this problem was remedied in time.

They also knew what to do about Kelly's obvious addiction to television. For the first couple of months they didn't turn it on except on very rare occasions, even though Kelly asked to watch almost incessantly. The most heartrending problem happened at night.

Olivia explained to me, "Kelly transitioned really well, but she did wake up screaming and crying in the night (night terrors) nearly every night for a few weeks. The bigger challenge was convincing her that she was allowed to come out of her bedroom. In the beginning, if we put her to bed she would just stay in her room no matter what, even if she needed to go to the bathroom or was scared or crying. It took about a month with us encouraging her and her getting closer to the doorway until she was eventually sitting in the doorway in the morning and finally sitting outside our door in the morning. We laugh that we have spent all the time since then trying to get her to stay in her room in the mornings (she is such an early riser)!"

As Kelly's CASA, I continued to visit her on a regular basis. My job wasn't complete until the case was closed. At times I still took Kelly to a park or the library or out for lunch. This would also give the "new" parents a little break, as they adjusted to being full-time parents to a three-year-old. Olivia worked out of the home during the day. Jim was able to be with Kelly in the daytime. In the evenings both parents were together with Kelly, except on occasion when Olivia traveled for work.

Whenever there was a court review, I wrote my report and let the judge know how Kelly was doing, what I thought of her new placement, and what things I hoped would happen for the best interest of this child. With every review, which in this case was happening about every sixty days, neither parent ever appeared. Grandmother was usually there and very verbal about why she wanted custody of her grandchild. She was quite upset every time she was told that would not be possible.

Having become a grandparent myself during this case, I understood how Grandmother was feeling; however, I was completely committed to watching over and keeping in mind the best interests of Kelly. I knew that this child wouldn't be safe with her biological family, and so I calmly, yet firmly, gave my opinion on this matter to all involved in the case.

In the meantime, I watched the love and closeness continue to develop between the Hewsons and Kelly.

Jim later related, "On the days when you visited, we had a fun routine. I would ask in a bad American accent, 'Who's that at the door, Kelly?' And Kelly would reply: 'Heeeeeer-rree's Ms. Bryant!'"

Each time I visited, I could see this child blossoming and growing in her safe and loving environment. I felt that I no longer needed to make weekly visits.

Sometimes before a visit I picked up tickets to an event around town. These tickets are donated to our CASA office. We then received an email about available tickets, and it would be a matter of first come, first served. These tickets were for the purpose of taking children to see things such as Disney on Ice, hockey games, or movies.

One day I picked up tickets for the nearby water park. I decided to let the Hewsons take Kelly to this attraction, instead of me. It was time to make the transition of slowly separating myself from Kelly and helping her become completely involved with her new family. The Hewsons were excited to share this experience with Kelly.

I sent an email to Olivia to see if they'd like to use these tickets with Kelly. Olivia wrote back:

"Jim and I had talked about taking Kelly to the water park before the summer ends, so the tickets sound great! Thank you for thinking of us! You're very welcome to stop by on Monday evening, if it isn't out of your way. We could also come by and pick them up from you, or meet somewhere. We'd love to tell you all about how Kelly is doing (excellent, great, lovely) and what a joy she is to have. You're welcome to call any evening to chat about Kelly too; even if we don't have anything specific to say, we're always glad to hear from you."

The Hewsons weren't aware that as a CASA volunteer we're instructed not to bring the children (or families) we're involved with to our own homes. For the sake of privacy this rule wasn't negotiable. I didn't feel the need for privacy where the Hewsons were concerned, but I followed procedure and told Olivia it wasn't a problem to bring the tickets to them. Besides, I was still visiting every other week or so, and the ticket drop off was a good reason for a visit.

Olivia also mentioned preschool in that same email:

"Kelly is starting preschool tomorrow (Mon, Wed, Fri from 8:30-11:00) so she picked out her clothes, blue since they are learning about blue this week, before she went to bed. She now has a playhouse outside and more toys and clothes than we know what to do with, thanks to our family and friends. Kelly has received several packages in the mail and loves to open them."

After five months with the Hewsons, it was apparent that Kelly's biological parents wouldn't be able to care for her. Discussions began with the Hewsons about whether they were interested in adopting Kelly.

"Interested" was the understatement of the year. Both Jim and Olivia could hardly contain their excitement. They loved Kelly from the first day they were together.

A court date was set for the "termination of parental rights." This procedure can be done with parents in court, where they sign over their rights of parental responsibility, and the child/children then become a ward of the county. In Kelly's case this procedure was done without the parents, as they were nowhere to be found.

The next step was to set a court date for final adoption. I will never forget the happiness I felt when I received this email, which also went out to Laura and Amber:

"It is with immense joy that we invite you to attend our Adoption Finalization Court Hearing ... on Wednesday, March 19, 2008 at 8:30 a.m.

Kelly has been with our family for a little over seven months and the entire experience has been nothing short of amazing. We count ourselves fortunate and privileged to have worked with all of you during this journey to our (expanding) forever family. We are humbled by the care you've shown not only for Kelly, but also for us as a family.

Therefore, we would be honored if you could join us at our adoption finalization court hearing. We're also planning to host an adoption celebration at our home later this month so please save the date March 29 — invitations will be coming soon.

Please RSVP and I'll make sure I send an update with the final location and any other relevant information for court."

I sent my RSVP the minute I read the email. I arrived a little early to court that day. As I waited in the hall, I thought about the Hewsons and Kelly and how happy the three of them must be feeling. Just then, I saw them enter the hallway. Olivia was looking radiant in her pink sweater and black skirt. Jim was wearing a black suit, complemented with a shiny, blue tie. Kelly was adorable in an aqua pinafore with pink roses to match her new mother's sweater. Instead of her usual white sandals, Kelly wore brand new, shiny, white, dress-up shoes.

If smiles could provide natural energy to a city, the four of us would've lit up New York City with no trouble!

Laura arrived shortly before the proceedings began. Amber had another court hearing, so Pam came in her place.

"Yolanda, we're so glad you're here with us today. Will you join us when this is over for a bite of lunch?" Olivia asked me as we waited for the judge.

"Of course; I'd be honored."

I stooped down to Kelly's level and asked, "Are you ready for this important day, Kelly?"

"Oh, yes, Ms. Bryant. I get to live with Jim and Olivia forever now!"

It was hard to keep the tears at bay, as I watched this mother and father become "official" parents. I made myself the designated picture taker, and realized that the whole courtroom was ours for this important moment. As a normal procedure adoptions are closed to the public, with the adopting family being the only ones to invite others to the proceedings.

When Judge Simmons entered the room, the four of us quickly stood. The judge smiled and asked us to be seated.

"Who is that you have with you today?" the judge asked Jim and Olivia as he took his seat.

"This is Kelly," Olivia answered.

"Kelly, that is a pretty name."

Kelly smiled at the judge.

As the judge turned his attention to the legal representatives, Pam and Laura introduced themselves. He then asked Jim and Olivia, as well as the caseworker, to please raise their right hands.

"Do you solemnly swear under the law that the testimony you are about to give in this matter is the truth, the whole truth, and nothing but the truth?"

"I do," said Jim, Olivia, and Pam.

"Do you believe Kelly is statutorily eligible for adoption by the petitioners?" the judge then asked the caseworker.

"Yes, your honor."

"Is this in her best interest?"

"Yes, it is."

"Does the agency consent?"

"Yes, we do."

"Thank you."

"Ms. Dumas (GAL), do you believe this is in the best interest of Kelly?"

"Yes, your honor."

"Thank you."

"All right. Olivia, are you able to meet Kelly's physical, educational, and emotional needs?"

"Yes, your honor."

"Can you provide her with a suitable home?"

"Yes, your honor."

"Financially provide for everybody who is dependent upon you for support?"

"Yes, your honor."

"Have you ever been on the child abuse registry?"

"No."

"Do you have any civil or criminal record?"

"No."

Through all of the questions, Kelly would wiggle a bit in her seat and turn now and then to look at those of us in the courtroom. However, she never made a sound. Jim and Olivia prepared her well for this special day.

The judge continued the procedure.

"Okay, I am showing her date of birth as December 7, 2003?"

"Yes, your honor."

"And how is she doing?"

"She is doing fantastic, your honor," Olivia said, turning and smiling at Kelly.

"That is good to hear."

Judge Simmons then turned his attention to Jim and asked the same questions of him. Jim was able to answer in the same way as Olivia.

The judge then looked out at Olivia's mother and myself.

"And for those family and friends that are here in attendance, should I grant this adoption?"

"Yes!" we both said heartily.

The judge chuckled at this point and commented, "I always get the same answer when I ask that."

He then took time to ask Kelly a few questions.

"How are you doing, Kelly?"

"Good."

"Are you in school?"

Kelly nodded her head in the affirmative, and looked to Olivia for clarification about school.

"Preschool," she said.

"Do you like it?"

"Yes."

"Do you have any pets — dogs, cats, fish, or anything?"

"Dogs."

"Really. What are their names?

"Merlin and Abba."

"Really. Are they nice dogs?"

"Yes."

"Good. All right."

The judge returned to the business at hand.

"The court finds that Kelly was born December 7, 2003. She does appear to be statutorily eligible for adoption by the petitioners. The petitioners appear to be of good moral character; they have the ability to support and educate Kelly and provide her with a suitable home. As for her mental and physical condition, Kelly does appear to be a proper subject for adoption by the petitioners. The best interests of Kelly will be served by the adoption. The best interest and welfare of Kelly will be promoted by the issuance of a final decree of adoption. It is therefore ordered by the judge that a final decree of adoption for Kelly is hereby granted. Her name is hereby changed to Kelly (k-e-l-l-y) Louise (l-o-u-i-s-e) Hewson (h-e-w-s-o-n). Said child shall be and is hereby entitled to all rights and privileges and subject to all obligations of a child pursuant to statute. I am signing the final decree of adoption at this time."

While the judge took a moment to sign this document, Kelly turned in her seat and gave a big smile to her little audience. Then the judge looked up from his paperwork.

"Congratulations," he said with a big smile. "You are a family."

We all began to clap. Jim and Olivia turned to smile, first at Kelly, and then at those of us watching this happy proceeding. Hugs quickly followed.

The judge stood, and with a big grin, motioned for this newly formed family to come forward for handshakes and more congratulations.

I sat quietly during the brief legal proceedings. As the judge finished his part and declared the Hewsons a family, I began taking pictures again.

"May we take our picture with you as well, judge?" Olivia quickly asked Judge Simmons.

"Of course. In fact, Kelly, why don't you come and sit right up here on my stand and we can take a picture from here."

I took several pictures of Kelly with the judge and her new mommy and daddy.

"We must get a few with you and Kelly as well, Yolanda," Olivia said.

I didn't need to be asked twice. As we left court, I watched a mother and a father and a little girl begin their lives as a forever family.

We went to a nearby Village Inn for lunch. While we waited for our orders, we reminisced about Kelly's journey.

"This is just the beginning of a wonderful story. I hope you'll keep in touch and let me know how the three of you are doing."

"We wouldn't have it any other way, Yolanda. As you know, we are having our party soon to officially welcome Kelly into the family. We hope that you and your husband can come to celebrate with us."

At the mention of the party, Kelly looked up from the coloring page she'd been given.

"Oh, yes, Ms. Bryant, you must come to my party!" she chimed in with a big grin.

"Of course I will, Kelly. I wouldn't miss it!"

As I drove home that day, my heart was full of gratitude: gratitude for the caseworker, the guardian ad litem, Jim and Olivia, and the CASA organization. Together, all of us worked to produce a miracle in the life of one young child. And that is how it is done, one child at a time.

Addendum to Kelly's Story

Jim and Olivia

The very first time we met Mrs. Bryant was when she (along with Kelly's GAL and caseworker) came to interview us after we submitted our application to foster-adopt Kelly. She was clearly very involved with Kelly and knew her as an individual. She asked us questions about ourselves but what we remember most was what she told us about Kelly.

From her, we learned about who Kelly was as a person: the types of activities she liked, her personality, her disposition, and her favorite things. She shared anecdotal stories that helped us to connect the information on paper to the little girl that we had never met but hoped would come to live with us. In short, she provided a window for us to see our future daughter.

With permission from the GAL and caseworker, Mrs. Bryant showed us a picture of Kelly. This small gesture (bringing a photo and volunteering to share it with us) brought tears to our eyes. As we walked around our home and chatted, she casually said things like, "Kelly loves dogs! I bet she would really like these dogs." A comment like that might seem trivial, but to us, it was a gift. We were nervous about the process, and as we had no other children, we were apprehensive and excited about becoming parents.

After the decision was made that Kelly would come to

live with us, it was Mrs. Bryant that called specifically to tell us that even though the caseworker and current foster home called her "Kellyann," she really preferred to be called Kelly. That she took the time to know and care about that small preference and share that with us to help ease the transition was so valuable.

Over the next six months, Mrs. Bryant continued to visit us as a family and to take Kelly on outings. She was considerate and respectful of us as a family but offered guidance and suggestions whenever asked. She was the transition from Kelly's first foster home, to us as a foster home, to us as an adoptive home.

Kelly came from a difficult circumstance with her birth parents to a foster home that presented its own challenges. Kelly always saw Mrs. Bryant as a nice lady that spent time with her and asked about her and how she was feeling. Even seven years later, Kelly still remembers the outings they took together and how warm and loved she felt with her.

During various court hearings, it was apparent that Mrs. Bryant's opinion and relationship with Kelly was respected and valued. I believe that Mrs. Bryant changed Kelly's life, as well as ours. Because of her, Kelly was always an individual person and not just another case. She helped to make sure that Kelly found a home that was a perfect fit for her, in real life and not just on paper, and she helped her transition to that home. To us, she was and will always be a dear family friend that is forever part of our family story.

Kelly

Hi! My name is Kelly and I'm going to tell you about my times with Mrs. Bryant. I'm very glad to tell you about it.

First of all, I remember that once she took me to a lake/pond sort of thing. The water was so clear. She tried to get me to get in, but I was scared. So I just dangled my feet in. I sort of regret not getting in, but I can have another time to paddle in the lake. So that was fun.

Next, she took me to Rattlesnake Hill and we walked and talked for a little bit. Luckily, there were no rattlesnakes when we went.

When she came over, I was really excited. I was always up for going out! There were so many places she took me. I was sad when I came back. Like the time she took me to my parents' (that I have now) house. I was crying because I didn't want to leave.

Lastly, I remember I felt really special to be going out with Mrs. Bryant, because she didn't take the other foster kids places. Even though I was sad for leaving my birth parents' house, she made me not think about it so much.

Postscript

As the years go by, I continue to hear from the Hewsons through emails and pictures. They eventually adopted a second child, Ava, from Russia, giving Kelly a sister. I hear about school, and how well Kelly does in her classes. I see pictures of Kelly with Merlin and Abba, and pictures of Kelly with Ava. My favorite pictures are of the happy, smiling faces of the whole family.

In 2012, I received this heartwarming email from Olivia:

"Here is a funny story. Recently, it came up in conversation with Kelly's third grade teacher that she is adopted. I mentioned that she came from foster care as a toddler. She was floored. In part, because she looks so much like me, but mostly, she just couldn't believe that a child that had a start like Kelly's could become one of her most courteous, treasured, and bright students (Kelly gets straight A's, of course). I bet she will be fascinated to read your story when you're done! Such a difference you made in Kelly's life. What would have happened to her if you hadn't been there watching out for her?!"

It reminded me once again of the reason I have continued to be a CASA volunteer. I have provided a strong and loving support to children who, through no fault of their own, find their lives turned upside down. No matter what kind of home a child comes from, the fact that strangers take them from all they know as family can be devastating. For a child, an advocate is a gift that can never be fully measured. To be an advocate is a gift I shall always treasure.

Visiting the CASA Playroom

At the Fair with Ms. Bryant

Adoption Day

Kelly never looked happier, and all of us involved in that special day couldn't keep from smiling.

Forever Home

Merlin and Abba became Kelly's instant friends.

Kelly with Ava, her new sister from Russia.

Besides being sisters, Kelly and Ava would become the dearest of friends.

The girls love to talk with a British accent, to copy Daddy.
Mommy is always proud to talk about the accomplishments of
her two beautiful daughters.

The Many Faces of CASA

Many people are unfamiliar with Court Appointed Special Advocates (CASA). This is a collection of thoughts and experiences shared by CASA volunteers. Many of these stories are by females, reflecting the ratio of women to men CASA volunteers. CASA is always hoping to find more men volunteers, as many children could benefit from the influence of a caring, adult male.

As mentioned in the story about Kelly, volunteers obtain thirty hours of training before they are given a case. The first and foremost thing we are taught as trainees is that the children and families with whom we work are entitled to complete privacy. This means we do not talk about names, places, or events while the case is in progress. The only person with whom we discuss details is our supervisor from the CASA office. Once a case is closed, if a family gives permission to share information, then doing so is acceptable (as in the story you just read about Kelly). We share some examples in the following pages. We reveal no specific details, although the cases for the most part are closed. We continue to respect the privacy of the children and the families.

One question we're often asked is, "How many hours a month does a volunteer devote to this work?" That's hard to answer, as each case is different. If a child is in a tough spot, having trouble in a placement or with another person, then visits may happen more than once a week. If a child's situation is stable and safe, then a weekly visit may be sufficient. After asking that same question to everyone that I interviewed, the number of hours per month averaged about eleven. What a small amount of time to make such a big difference in the life of a child!

After volunteers are trained, they are required to get twelve hours of continuing education credit per year. Credit may be earned by reading a relevant book and discussing it in a group, viewing a movie on subjects chosen by the CASA office, or being invited to trainings given throughout the county for caseworkers, guardians ad litem, and volunteers. We obtain many valuable tools for working effectively with children and with adults that may suffer physical, mental, and emotional handicaps. Volunteers find these tools helpful in every aspect of life, whether working with others, or in the home.

One CASA remarked, "I feel bad that with my work schedule and then giving my time to my little CASA guy, I've only participated in a couple of training sessions."

My response to her was: "You shouldn't feel bad at all. The most important thing you can do is be a part of that child's life. They could care less what 'special training' you take. They are just thrilled that you are in their life and that they have someone they can count on. It doesn't take training to know how to love."

Stephanie

I love children and don't have any of my own, so when I heard about this organization and the people that were making a difference in children's lives, the thought that I could be a part of this excited me. I wanted to help make a difference in a child's life. The stories that I heard from my friend were what inspired me to join. I heard stories of children coming from terrible situations and going into new, loving families. I saw pictures of the children smiling, even after all the pain they suffered. These children inspired me and made me want to be a part of CASA.

I have been Sam's CASA for about three years now. One of the things we've consistently done on visits is enjoy a meal together, along with some other activities. When I first met Sam, he was very introverted and shy and had a hard time even speaking to people. When we'd go to restaurants, many times I'd order for him, because speaking made him nervous. In time he overcame his shyness. He also has wonderful manners now. He consistently tells people, "Yes, please" or "No, thank you."

At a visit to the Red Robin restaurant, he ordered his meal and said, "Yes, please" and "Thank you" to the waitress. She made a special point to thank Sam for having such great manners. She told him it was refreshing to meet a young person as well-mannered as he was. His reply was "Thank you." He smiled the rest of the meal.

Recently I showed up at the Boys & Girls Club to pick up Sam for a visit. As we were leaving the building, he said, "I have to get my bike. It's locked up outside."

I replied, "What? Your bike?"

Sam was close to fourteen years old then, and he had never been taught to ride a bike. So the fact that he was riding a bike was quite shocking.

We got to the bench where his bike was waiting. He had a lock with a combination, a helmet, and an impressive white mountain bike. It was the kind of bike any young man would be proud to ride.

After Sam unlocked his bike, we headed toward the restaurant, which wasn't far away. I was walking along so I could watch Sam with his bike. He hopped on and took off. He would ride up a block, then ride back to meet me, all the while with a big grin on his face.

Sam and I had talked about bikes many times before in the last three years, and he always insisted he was too afraid to learn. Yet there he was, riding a bike down the sidewalk all by himself. Sam told me he taught himself about three weeks prior to this visit.

"What made you decide to learn after all this time?" I asked.

"I got tired of being the only one in my group of friends who couldn't ride a bike to the park. So one day I just decided to teach myself."

The determination and pride that Sam showed made that particular visit one to remember. This young man who had suffered so much in his short life was already proving to himself that he could overcome obstacles.

I have been a volunteer for almost four years now. I'm now more tolerant of people in general. Getting a glimpse into other people's lives has taught me not to judge so quickly. I now understand why adults and children alike act certain ways. I'm more confident in my ability to advocate on behalf of CASA children. I've learned that these kids, who have endured so much pain, are still just kids who like to laugh, to play, and to have fun.

One part of this work that concerned me at first was the writing of reports. The court reports can be challenging, because I want to give only accurate data. But I know reports are necessary to provide the best representation of the facts on behalf of the children.

I appreciate the chance to go to court, because I enjoy being the voice for the child. I enjoy being able to express what the child needs and desires to a room full of professionals. It's empowering to know that you're representing a child who can't represent himself. Initially, I was nervous to speak in front of a bunch of people. However, when I remember that I'm advocating on a child's behalf, speaking is much easier and my nervousness goes away pretty quickly.

In working with the caseworkers and the guardians ad litem, I met several professionals who are passionate about children and what they're doing. I don't always agree with the decisions made by these professionals, but I feel as if they are respectful when listening to my point of view. The court magistrates listen to what I say. They always thank the CASA for the work we do and for the hours we spend on the case. They make me feel proud of the work that we've done. The work isn't always easy, because you sometimes see and hear terrible things. These things affect you, making it meaningful to hear even a simple "thanks" from the legal people.

Another group of people with whom we work are the foster families. In general, the foster families I work with are receptive to my questions and to my interactions with their foster children. I encountered only one especially difficult foster mother. Though this woman knew what a CASA was, she refused to answer my questions or cooperate in any way, even refusing to let me see where her foster child slept. I did discover she had been a foster parent for more than twenty years. This may have been part of the reason she seemed tired and out of sorts. She told me once, "I know how things are with these kids, and I don't take crap from any of them." This attitude translated to my CASA child rarely getting in trouble, but he also never received a good word or compliment from this foster mother.

At times, my biggest concern is with the parents of my children. The reason behind that is you are dealing with children who have been abused or neglected. You read reports about the allegations against these parents, and it's easy to form an opinion about the parents before you meet them. This can make it hard to be unbiased when you need to speak to them. I handle it by trying to be caring to the parents. The ones I encountered had rough lives themselves and are trying to do the best they can. One mother was living in poor conditions and sharing the place with another lady. I decided to take a pizza one night when I went to visit. I wanted them to feel that I was aware of their struggles and willing to help with this small gesture of bringing dinner. In trying to get the father to open up, I arranged our visits to take place at a Starbucks, where I could at least buy him a cup of coffee. In that case, I was the first person to show genuine interest in his feelings and not just see him as the bad guy. In fact, in time, everyone involved in the case began to see that Dad really had more going for him than initially reported. In doing this work, I try my best to use empathy and put myself in each person's shoes.

The children you meet as a CASA will change your life. I went into this because I wanted to help … but many times I feel I learn more from the children than they learn from me. These children will inspire you and teach you how to be stronger yourself. Due to the nature of the cases, you'll have hard days and maybe even shed some tears of sadness. However, the first time the child says something like, "Thank you for being nice to me," you'll be fully committed.

Anita

Recently I was speaking with the adoptive mother of a little girl for whom I had advocated. She told me that there was an honor that her older brother's school had instituted at graduation. This honor was to go to someone who made an impression in your life who was not a relative.

My little kiddo turned to her mother and said, "I know who I will give that honor to when it's my turn."

"And who would that be?" the mother asked.

"My CASA, Anita."

Those kinds of comments make all your work worthwhile.

I'm on my ninth case now and I feel very lucky. Except for one case, each child was placed with a family I felt was the best possible one for them. I keep in touch with most of the children, so I'm confident in the placement. Once you are in their lives, it's hard to drop out of sight.

My hardest case lasted five years. There were five children. Dealing with the parents was challenging. I didn't realize how much the parents were abusing the children until much later. Since I'm stubborn and have the law on my side, I was able to see the children weekly at my convenience. Ideally the abusive parents have consequences without hurting the children in the process. In this case, the abuse was much worse than anyone thought. The caseworker removed the children. This was after many visits and with many agencies assisting the children. They had to be split into three foster homes.

The youngest went to a good foster home and flourished there. Then a relative adopted her, and she remains there today. The oldest two were placed in a foster home that didn't work, and they were moved to another foster home. Neither one of these homes was good for the children. However, we kept thinking that the case would close. Was it worth moving them?

In the latter home, the older two were able to see their siblings at school each day. I was so happy and relieved when these two were all moved to a permanent home with relatives.

The middle two children went to a foster home where they learned prejudice. They were there for more than a year before moving to their aunt's home, where they were adopted. This aunt and uncle also adopted the eldest two. This meant that, overnight, the aunt and uncle went from having one child, their own biological daughter, to having five children. This case was also difficult because the placement was out of state. Sadly, though, soon after the children were adopted, their aunt and uncle got a divorce.

The final outcome was that the four older ones are together and are living with a woman who has all my respect and admiration. Imagine trying to fit seven people into one car? All their lives changed immediately. To further complicate these kids' lives, the aunt is now overseas, because she's serving in the United States Army. The children are in a permanent home and have good relatives surrounding them, though they continue to have problems due to the former abuse.

When I get frustrated with the way things go at times, I keep remembering that I'm there for the kids. We make sure their welfare, their safety, and their future are our only priority. If there is a concern, I go to my boss at the CASA office. Sometimes she decides on a solution; and sometimes we just talk it out.

I enjoy working with the court representatives. All my experiences so far have been positive. I work with several different caseworkers and guardians ad litem. One in particular has proven to be loyal, honest, and fun. We work well together. All of the legal people treat me with respect and show appreciation for my work. Every magistrate I've known has been impressive. Deciding a child's fate within the boundaries of the law while accommodating the parents must be difficult. On the other hand, it often frustrates me, because when I realize the situation I want the judge or magistrate to place the children immediately where I believe they need to be.

I will always be glad my son came home from a CASA fundraiser and decided to call and tell me all about it. I would say to those of you thinking about this work, CASAs are so needed. Be strong! It will enrich your life.

Kevin

Justin is five years old. His eight-year-old brother was moved to Florida in December 2013 to live with their maternal grandmother. Justin is living with their paternal grandparents. Justin and Jared were removed from their home in February 2013, and I've been their CASA since March 2013.

In spite of not seeing his mother for almost eighteen months, seeing his father only once or twice a week, and his brother living in Florida, Justin still remains happy, loving, and positive. When I go to see him or pick him up, he always asks about my daughter, who he's met numerous times. He always wants to go play arcade games or go to see a movie. When I leave after a visit, I'm always speechless when he yells out, "Love you, Mr. Kevin!" as he runs into the house. This little five-year-old boy has taught me more about strength and a positive attitude than a hundred books ever could.

Fortunately, in working my cases, the two foster families were wonderful to the children and kept me well informed of their status. I especially appreciated this when I was out of town for work assignments. Foster parents are truly heroes to the kids in their care and their opinions should be valued much more than they are at times.

I understand that the caseworkers and guardians ad litem

are burdened with a lot of cases; however, I find that they generally approach cases with little urgency and with little regard for the opinions of the foster parents or the CASA. During court, I dislike hearing the acronyms thrown around about each child's case and the social-work language that is used so clinically regarding each child and their case. I do feel, though, that the magistrate truly wants to hear my opinions.

I heard about this work through a friend and have been a CASA for almost three years. In other capacities, I worked with kids for years. Then I found this organization where I thought I really could impact a child's future. After learning more, I realized that the children in the welfare system experienced the worst hardships imaginable and were in desperate need of help to bring stability and safety to their lives. Now that I've been a CASA for a while, I think the work is even more important than I initially thought. We have no other motivation than each child's safety and welfare — something that isn't necessarily true of others involved in the children's cases.

In one of my cases, I dealt with a child, his mother, and his grandmother. After one year, the son was returned to his mother. I felt this outcome was appropriate and that the mother truly attempted to turn her life around, with the help of the grandmother's permanent intervention in their lives.

My advice about this volunteer work is to do it with a passion for helping a child. Do not fear giving your opinion to any professional at any time. They can do nothing to you, but you can do a lot for a child in need.

Andrea

I had the privilege of being the CASA volunteer for Lacy, age four, for the past twenty months. One June afternoon, I arrived at Lacy's foster home at one p.m. to take her to a petting zoo. I rang the doorbell and Lacy's foster mom quickly opened the door and greeted me. I saw Lacy peeking around the corner of the staircase.

"My Andrea!" she cried, running towards me and giving me a huge hug. "We're going to have fun today!"

Even though Lacy said these exact words nearly every time I picked her up, I never tired of hearing her tell me how much fun we are going to have together or of hearing her call me "my Andrea."

"Hi, Lacy! We are going to have fun! I can't wait to hang out with you! I love your purple leggings and flower T-shirt."

"She got ready at eight a.m. because she was so excited to go to the petting zoo with you. And then she picked out her own outfit, because she said she remembered your favorite color was purple."

Being Lacy's friend and advocate gave me so much joy in my life.

At sixteen, I was volunteering at Tennyson Center for Children through a service project organized by my high school. It was this experience that made me aware of my passion for helping abused and neglected children. A couple of years ago, I googled volunteer opportunities with children and stumbled across the CASA website. When I heard about CASA, also known as Advocates for Children, I knew this was something that I had to do. I went through training a week later.

I've never volunteered for something where my input is as valued as it is in my CASA work. The court reports are a crucial element in advocating for the kids I represent. It's the only way to get our recommendations and concerns heard in the courtroom. I enjoy writing these reports because I know the magistrate and many other professionals who are making crucial, life-altering decisions regarding these kids' futures will read them.

Except for court running late and waiting at length for some of my cases to be called, I love participating in these hearings. I like bragging about my CASA kids when things are going well, and I also think it's necessary for all of the professionals to hear mine and others' concerns when something isn't going well. I think it's helpful to have all of the decision makers in one room along with the magistrate. The court hearings are a good time to attempt to keep everyone on the same page regarding the case.

Lacy's foster family was amazing They welcomed me into their home every time and were respectful and understanding of the legal process. My experience with this foster family made me grateful that Lacy had a placement like this one.

Being a CASA volunteer, I constantly am reminded how strong these kids are. They are survivors. They've been through things most adults never experience, and yet, at the end of the day, they're still just kids who want to be kids. My feelings changed toward this work in the sense that I now focus on seeing my CASA kiddos as children and not as victims of abuse. Their experiences shape the people they are becoming, but their abuse and neglect don't define them. They're children with personalities, goals, dreams, likes, dislikes, and desires. I feel I'm a better CASA volunteer when I'm able to focus on these parts of my kiddos.

I want to finish by giving this advice: Trust your instincts. If something feels off, it probably is. And never feel like you're alone! The CASA staff offers much guidance and is always helpful in working with you through your cases.

Bryan

Although I am a new CASA volunteer, having just started a little over a year ago, I watched my mother do this work. She became a volunteer when she retired. I knew I wanted to do something meaningful, and since I love kids, CASA seemed a perfect fit. I found that I love this work even more than I thought I would. Sure, going to court isn't something I particularly enjoy, because it's a sad time. Nobody is there for a happy reason. Still, I know it's important to go. I'm continually amazed by the quality of people and the time everybody takes to help. There are some unbelievably generous and wonderful caseworkers and guardians ad litem in the world. Sometimes you have to get into some ugly situations to see it. I think the magistrates do an amazing job of working through a lot of information to get to the truth and make decisions as fairly as possible.

With my first case, I felt conflicted, because I wanted the father and mother to do what they were supposed to do. I was truly rooting for them, but it's pretty heartbreaking to see them say one thing and then do another. I'd try and stay focused on the children. One thing I always emphasize with my CASA kiddos is education. Every time I would go and pick up the three kids, ages six, seven, and nine, I'd ask them how things were going in school, how they'd done in class and on recent tests, etc. Though they were totally bewildered by these questions initially and weren't sure whether I was serious or how to answer them, I think I got an important message across. I remember a conversation I had with one of the children about the third time I'd gone and taken them for a fun activity.

"Bryan, what's the day after tomorrow?" the child asked.

"The day after tomorrow is Wednesday," I answered.

"Could you come back and pick us up tomorrow … and

Wednesday ... and ... and ... all the rest of the days?" she asked.

It was very funny and heartwarming to know she really wanted to be with me.

I wanted to be sure these children had someone telling them that learning and working hard in school is extremely important, and that they could do it. At first they just wanted to listen to the radio or some of the old-school hip-hop I played for them. They were particularly fond of Run-DMC. They also were interested in whatever fun activity I planned, but I insisted that on the way to the activity they each had to tell me how things were going and three things they learned in school. If they did, then we could have some fun and sing along to some appropriate old-school hip-hop.

After they shared their achievements in school and things they learned, I would praise them and emphasize that they were smart kids and that, if they worked hard in school, they could be the best in their class and do anything they wanted. For me, the most gratifying thing was that after a while they stopped insisting on listening to music right away or chatting about whatever and instead would volunteer all the things that they were learning in school and how well they were doing and so on. It was especially great to see all three kids saying, "I am good at math" or "I am really smart at science," because without that positive belief in themselves it's not very likely that they'll achieve great things. It was wonderful to see them stating these affirmations out loud and believing that they could and should do well in school. The kids were unbelievable throughout the case, and the happy result is that grandmother and grandfather are moving toward adopting three wonderful grandchildren.

My advice to those wanting to be a CASA is: Do it! Just try it. It sounds harder than it is. Not that it isn't hard — but you get through the hard stuff, and you help the kids get through it, and you're all better for it. It's an amazing and rewarding experience. The three CASA children I've been lucky enough to get to know are one hundred percent awesome!

Josiane

I was privileged to be a CASA volunteer for Lucas for the last three years, starting when he was just three months old. His mother was a meth addict at the time her case was opened. We thought she was recovering, as the most important thing in her life was to get on track so that she could reunite with her son. During a supervised Valentine's Day outing with the two of them, his mom had a meth-withdrawal incident, which led me to notify the Department of Human Services. The decision was made to have all visits supervised by myself at DHS rather than to have public outings. During one of my supervised visits at DHS, I approached the mother with a hug, as I always do, after having just picked up baby Lucas from his foster home. He was then eight months old.

"Hi. How are you doing?" I asked her.

"I can't do this anymore," she said, putting her head on my shoulder and beginning to cry. "I need help. Where can I go?"

"Are you saying you want to go to rehab for your addiction?"

"Yes. I thought it would be easier, and it's not."

"I want to help you and see you succeed so you and Lucas can be together. Let me make some phone calls to see what is available for you."

"Thank you so much. I don't have a lot of people in my life that can help me. I just am done failing."

"You have a team that wants you to succeed for your sake and your son's. Be strong. I will call you tomorrow with what options you may have. Right now, hug and love your baby."

I researched rehabilitation centers right away. I learned the many rehab opportunities for her. However, before we could get something arranged, the mother disappeared and was on the run for three weeks. Because she couldn't make changes for so long, her parental rights were terminated. His loving foster family, who had cared for him since he was three months old, adopted little Lucas. The good news is that his biological mother eventually turned herself in and was put in a program where, to this day, she is clean of her addiction.

I got started with CASA about eight years ago. While I was researching the possibility of going to law school, I ran across information about this organization. I had a child development degree that I used for only two years and then decided to go back to school for a business degree and then pursue a career in high technology. I always missed doing something that was child-oriented. Coupled with my interest of going to law school, I thought this was a good way to engage both interests. I do enjoy going to court. Every time I go I learn something new. Being part of a legal team provides a clear view of what outcomes to expect. At times, going to court puts families in a position of uncertainty, which can cause a lot of emotional distress. I've been fortunate to be able to work with many fabulous caseworkers and guardians ad litem. I'm often able to work with the same people on several cases; this makes the court process easier. One thing that's great about our magistrate is that she was a CASA herself while going to law school, so we always feel that she respects our role in court and, more importantly, that she reads our reports.

My advice to those considering this work is to use all of the resources that are available to you and don't be afraid to ask questions.

Shondra

I was drawn to my last case for a personal reason. This teenage boy for whom I chose to advocate had the same type of brain surgery that I'd undergone recently. Unfortunately, he suffered a stroke from the surgery and was left mentally handicapped. He also was in the foster-care system, and things weren't being done properly for his special needs. I instantly became not only his advocate, but also a "lion in his corner." I can get very vocal, and when I felt this young man was being overlooked or shuffled off to the easiest option, I let people know that was wrong.

Now, I will say that I've been impressed with the foster families I've gotten to know. They've not been in it for the money, but they genuinely cared about the children they fostered. However, the system has failed to give these great foster families the support they need. Social Services would tell them time and again, "Oh, we'll get to that. We'll let you know." Often, however, the families would be left hanging.

At times I almost walked away from this work, because I was so upset with the way the system was run and with the decisions that were made for my special-needs child. One part of my brain understands the many cases that each social worker and each guardian ad litem has to review. However, the mother side of me says, "I don't care how many cases someone has; this child is important and I want everyone involved to give him the time and attention he deserves, so that the best choices can be made on his behalf." In time, I would find some hope when the magistrate listened to what I had to say in advance of making final decisions.

I also remind myself, when I am feeling discouraged about my ability to help this young man, that I was led to CASA by a power higher than mine. I had been praying to know what

God would have me do to reach out to others. It was then that I remembered some handouts I'd received about CASA, and shortly thereafter I received an email from Stacey, a supervisor at CASA, about some upcoming training. I knew I'd been led to an opportunity I couldn't ignore.

Whenever I talk to a gentleman friend about doing this work, I tell him first how much CASA needs more men to volunteer. So many children could be influenced for good by a strong male role model. I also tell him you always have to stay focused on the child. Don't be discouraged by the politics. It's the child that needs you. As with the young man in my last case, if I didn't speak up for him, who would? Also, make sure to take notes about everything that happens with your case. Keep things well documented. And for heaven's sake, don't be afraid to fight the system when it's needed!

Marty

I was at a volunteer fair in Colorado when I found out about CASA. I saw this organization as an on-going, in-the-trenches way to make a positive impact.

In one of my cases, I found it extremely easy to work with the foster family. They welcomed me into their home and let me see the children anytime I wanted. Dealing with the children's parents was both frustrating and rewarding. I was able to facilitate enrichment activities for the boys, which one or the other has attended, such as zoo and museum visits, trampoline facility outings, and biking and playground activities. I had the chance to coach the parents and model some parenting skills for them. Finally, I helped them think long term in regard to their own lives and the lives of their children. The granddad has supported his daughter well, and both grandparents welcomed me into their children's lives.

The caseworkers and guardians ad litem were responsive throughout my case. I was a little frustrated with stipulations that kept changing. For example, the grandmother was not allowed private time with the children; now the children are living in their grandparents' home along with their mother. Also, the mother was supposed to get independent housing, and yet the professionals are now allowing her to live with her mom and dad.

I think court is especially good for a mother or father, as the hearing can be a reward session, or if a parent has not been complying with court orders, a reality check. I feel that the parent listens more to what the court magistrate tells them than to what anyone else tells them.

My advice is get to know all the people involved in your case, including the children, parents, foster parents, relatives, guardians ad litem, caseworkers, parenting time workers, support services people, educational and therapy support people. The more you can know the total situation, the better you can advocate for the child.

Alan and Tammy

We learned about CASA through an ad in the newspaper. We've been volunteers for two years. We wanted to make a difference in the lives of children. It's beneficial to work as a team for our children. A man and a woman have perspective as a couple that makes life's decisions balance. We're able to make decisions as if they were our own children. In our last case, the two girls with whom we worked didn't seem to favor one of us over the other. Both girls were polite and well-behaved. We enjoyed spending time with them. Alan is a great negotiator and was able to set up a lot of free activities that we could enjoy with the children. I'm the one that takes all the notes and writes the court reports.

From the start CASA volunteering was rewarding. The first time we visited and shared with the girls who we were and what we wanted to do for them, you should've seen the looks on their faces. "TT," the older sibling, had a look of sheer wonderment. Being able to watch the growth and development in both of them was tremendously satisfying. Just telling them how valuable they are and seeing them start to believe in themselves is awesome. For example, TT was afraid of stuffed animals at the museum. Even bugs on the sidewalk would cause fear. But all of that is now a thing of the past. It's amazing how much love and trust can make a difference in a person's life.

At times, we were disillusioned by caseworkers or guardians ad litem that act as if it's just a job to them. However, we were quite impressed by the court magistrate who swore us in as new CASA volunteers. He helped us see how important this work could be and the difference we could make for a child.

In working with the foster families, we wish we saw the families treating the foster children more as they would want to be treated themselves.

As the mother of two, I know how important it is for siblings to spend time together. It breaks my heart knowing how close my children are and realizing how many siblings in the foster system must spend time apart. Seeing how much joy it brings our two CASA children to be together makes it all worth the time we spend.

Alan: Each of us as CASAs, or foster families, or the legal people, should be doing this for the children. If I were one of those children, I would like to think someone would help me. We have this opportunity to make a difference for eternity in someone's life. Everyone needs someone to believe in him.

Emily

While attending university, I participated in an internship as a victim advocate for the local sheriff's department. I shared an office space with the Advocates for Children staff from Douglas County, Colorado. I got to know Caroline and Marcia pretty well and shadowed them for a time during my internship. I knew that once I graduated and turned twenty-one, I would volunteer with them. I grew up with a love for volunteer work, as my parents were in public service. My mother has been a victim advocate for close to twenty years now, and my father has been in law enforcement for about the same time. Growing up, I felt I had a blessed life with a great family. If I could help others who weren't so fortunate to have a loving home, then I wanted to do whatever I could. Also, I love kids and wanted to be as involved with them as I could be.

When it comes to writing court reports, I actually don't mind that task. In fact, I think I wrote a couple more reports than I needed to. I remember once staying up until about one in the morning to turn in a report on time, only to find out that I was over a month early. Now I find the report-writing process almost therapeutic. It can help me to focus my energy on my case and identify different ways to advocate for the kids.

What goes on in court is always interesting. Seeing how well all of the professionals know their cases is pretty amazing. I have a single case at a time, and I always feel as if I may have missed something. I'm constantly in awe of how well the caseworkers and guardians ad litem keep up with their many cases. The court magistrate has to be on top of all the cases. It blows my mind that they can keep up with all the information. The only thing that's hard for me in court is speaking on the record. I'm nervous that I'm going to call the magistrate "Your Majesty" or "Sir" instead of "Ma'am." I haven't done that yet. Knock on wood.

There's one case that I think of often, and it will always remind me of why I continue to be a CASA volunteer. I was assigned to this case after the parents' rights had been terminated and all three children were available for adoption. After the parents were no longer involved in the case, it was interesting to see how the other relatives became inconsistent influences in the children's lives and wishy-washy about being placement providers. I felt that the relatives were determined to be placement providers when the parents were involved, but it later came out that they only acted that way with the intention either to allow frequent contact with the parents or to give the children back to the parents. When they were told that this wasn't allowed to happen, suddenly other things came up in their lives that made them unable to care for the kids.

The children were remarkably resilient during this case, even though they knew what was going on. For example, the children were aware that biological relatives had agreed to take them after their parents' rights were terminated. The children began living their lives as if they weren't going to be in their foster home the next day and often would tell people about it. One time, I was arranging a visit for the siblings to get together to plan for one of the children's birthdays a couple of weeks later. The children didn't want to plan anything with me, anticipating they would have moved to their relatives' home in another state by that time. It was about four months later that the relatives took back their decision to have the children placed with them. The children then went through the heartache of being rejected by family members.

However, after seven months of being available for adoption, I had the honor of participating in an adoption presentation meeting for my three CASA kids. An adoption presentation meeting occurs after a family approaches the Department of Human Services about adopting children from foster care, passes their home study, and talks with the department about the different children who are up for adoption. This is the first meeting that the caseworker, guardian ad litem, and for this case, myself, present all the nitty-gritty information about the adoptable children to prospective adoptive parents. This includes presenting thorough family, medical and dental, developmental, and academic histories, along with the history of the dependency and neglect case.

After the case worker reported the difficult portion of the information to the prospective adoptive parents about thirteen-year-old Derek, eleven-year-old Katrina, and nine-year-old Carter, it was time to talk about the fun stuff that made these three the adorable kids that they were. At that point in the meeting, the caseworker turned the time over to me by saying, "No one knows these kids like Emily does. She will be able to really bring these three to life for you. She loves these kids, and everyone knows how much they love her!"

At that point, I delved into the fun stuff, beginning with Derek.

"Derek absolutely loves football. He eats, sleeps, and breathes it! If you simply give him your ear, he'll tell you more about football than you even knew existed."

"Oh, my gosh, our son is on the varsity football team!" exclaimed the potential adoptive mother. "He's dying for someone to talk to about football too!"

"Now, Katrina is such a girly girl," I revealed. "She loves to get her nails done and always wants everyone to get theirs done too."

With a huge grin on his face, the potential adoptive father elbowed his wife. "Now Katrina definitely will fit in nicely with the girls."

"My daughter and I have a standing 'date' every weekend to get our nails done," his wife added.

"Lastly, the sweetest thing about Carter is his love of

T-shirts. He only wants to wear T-shirts, loves taking the promo T-shirts at different events, and that's all he wants to spend his money on. On top of that, he organizes them by color in his closet."

Now it was the potential adoptive mother, wide-eyed and crying, nudging her husband.

"Wow," he exclaimed. "That's exactly like me. Man, if he isn't destined to be my son, I don't know who is. That is my son, one hundred percent."

Only a few short weeks after this meeting, Derek, Katrina, and Carter began calling these two "Mom" and "Dad."

Watching what children like these have endured makes my closing advice close to my heart. My perspective comes from someone who doesn't have children of her own, but I have many children in my life. You would never want your child, niece or nephew, student, neighbor, brother or sister, or church member to be abused or neglected. Heaven forbid they ever were, but if it happened you would want someone to be there for them and to get to know them really well. You would believe that they deserved someone to help them feel as normal as possible, to identify a safe and stable home, to help them realize that there are trustworthy and good examples in adults, and to help them live a happy life. Well, each of these kids is someone's niece or nephew, student, neighbor, sibling, church member, or child. Don't they deserve the same?

Stacey

My co-CASA and I had two of our five kids in the car for an outing to get frozen yogurt. The two oldest were in the backseat, and the seven-year-old said she really wanted to "go home to mommy right now" and kept repeating that. Her big sister told her to stop because everybody knew that. She also said that no one was doing anything to help her mother get them back. When I told her that we were trying to help her mom, she said with quite a bit of frustration, "No, you're not!" It broke my heart.

When we arrived at the frozen yogurt place, my co-CASA took the seven-year-old inside so I could talk to Talia. We sat down on a bench, and I asked her to look at me, which she wouldn't do. I gently put both my hands on either side of her head and turned her face so I could look her in the eye. I promised her that we were helping her mommy try and get them home. I told her that I knew her mommy loved her very much and that she loved her mommy. I told her that we wanted all the kids to go home to their mommy. I could tell by the look in her eyes that she didn't believe me.

"You don't believe me, do you?" I asked her, and she said no. I told her that was okay and that we would keep helping her mommy any way we could.

The two older children have returned home, and they're doing well. I followed up with Talia.

"I told you that we wanted you to go home to your mommy and that she was working hard to get you home."

She smiled.

I heard about CASA twenty years ago when I was working at a halfway house for adult felony offenders. Some of their kids had CASA volunteers. Ever since I heard about CASA, I wanted to become a volunteer. Life circumstances didn't give me that opportunity for many years. Three years ago, I was laid off as the general manager of Borders Books when the company closed. I decided it was time to return to my human-services roots both personally and professionally. I decided to go through the CASA training.

Having been a volunteer for several years, I now believe that there are more good people in this world than bad and that those good people want to help kids. I believe that parents do not plan to abuse their kids and that there's something redeemable in every parent. I believe even more strongly that CASA volunteers are amazing people and that we make a difference in the lives of the children we serve.

When I think about the many people with whom we work as volunteers, it strikes me how differently people view the phrase, "best interest of the child." My CASA work requires that I take a lot of deep breaths. I try to see everyone's side and then try to determine if there's a way we can come to a consensus. I don't have a problem speaking my mind when it comes to the welfare of a child, so sometimes I just jump right in, which works more often than not to get the ball rolling.

An example of this determination happened with the five kids I mentioned earlier. The two middle ones were in a foster home with three biological children of the foster parents and an adopted baby. The home was very chaotic, as all of the children were home-schooled. Our two kids had severe eczema. The foster family had never dealt with eczema before. My co-CASA brought the foster parents products for their hair and skin specifically made for eczema. Both parents were given instructions on how to use the products. Yet it was a constant battle to get the foster family to properly treat the eczema. We routinely saw the kids with painfully dry and cracked skin.

The final straw was when we saw the kids during visitation with their mom at the Department of Human Services. Both kids had very dry and cracked skin, which was also bleeding. Clearly they weren't receiving proper care. My co-CASA and I had the caseworker look at the kids. We called the guardian ad litem's office, and we insisted the kids be removed that day. The caseworker called the on-call supervisor, who agreed with our plan. The foster mother who had the two older girls agreed to care for the two middle children until they could be moved to a relative's home a week later. They moved that very day.

That case lasted two and a half years. The two oldest, ages eight and seven, finally were returned home to mom. A paternal cousin adopted the youngest, age two. The two middle kids, who were four and six, were granted permanent allocation of parental rights to a different paternal relative.

This case has far more challenges and delays than is typical, and I believe the children paid the price for that. There's no doubt in my mind that having co-CASA volunteers on this case made a world of difference for those five kids.

My advice to other volunteers is to be patient and know that, even though you can't see it all of the time, you do make a difference in the lives of children. Trust that your influence will be felt long after the cases close.

Shanelle

I was Stacey's co-CASA on the case that was shared previously. I learned about the organization through a friend, who was also a co-worker. At the time I was attending school and studying criminal justice. My friend kept telling me I should be a CASA. I told her that I would look into it when I got out of school. I have been a volunteer since 2011.

The education I received in criminal justice helped me in

working with the caseworkers and guardians ad litem. I can't say that part of the work is easy, but I feel I had some training that helps with the legal people. The communication with them at times is frustrating, but it helps me to understand what they go through. And I realize it is very necessary as a CASA to be able to work well with the legal people. I find this the most difficult part of being a volunteer.

On one level, you have the emotions of dealing with the children and the foster families, but the details involved in dealing with the professionals is the hardest part for me. The actual court reports aren't hard for me. I appreciate the several people in the CASA office that go through the report before it's submitted to court. It's good to have this documentation to go back to when we're working on a case. I know some people are frustrated with reports, as paperwork is never the fun part, but I know that they're necessary. I think writing the reports also reminds you that you aren't just hanging out with a child and buying him or her an ice cream, but that what you're doing is serious. You're recording information to help this child.

I have appreciated a co-CASA for the main reason that two heads and two hearts are better than one. I caught things that she didn't catch, and she caught things that I didn't catch. At times, there were different feelings on some things, so it was good to share our different perspectives. I feel like the case got even better attention for having two different people looking at it. At times if one of us couldn't do something, the other one was able to pick up the slack.

Now, as the case is over for us, sitting here thinking about it, I wouldn't have guessed in a million years that it would've wound up as it did. I honestly think it was the right outcome, which means I'm able to sleep at night. Having said that, I must say that this case took a big toll on me for many reasons. In our two and a half years on this case we had two different guardians ad litem and four different caseworkers. I was grateful for the CASA training that I received before starting my case, as it reminded me that the ultimate goal in our work is to focus on the safety of these children and to help them find the best support system available to them.

You sometimes get wrapped up in thinking about what you personally feel is best for these kids, but that may not ideally be what can happen for them. I constantly thought back on "what is the safest option for this child." That really helped me to do my best in this work. So, coupled with the fact that I have just had my first child, I will be taking a break from CASA for a while. In the future, I may decide to take another case.

I would love to team with Stacey again. She was a wonderful co-CASA. We balanced each other. I kept things cut and dried when I felt I was being emotionally bulldozed, and she was protective of the kids. Stacey's passion for the kids needed to be there to help us complement one another. I think we did our job very well as a team. Many times we were sure that things wouldn't end positively for the children. However, by the end of the case, we were both grateful for the outcome and that it was the right one for these children.

The best advice I would give to someone considering doing this work is: don't feel pressured to take on a particular case. If it doesn't feel right to you, don't feel like you have to take it. You get to make the decision on which cases you will take. Listen to what your heart is telling you, because I don't feel you can help any situation or any child if you yourself aren't prepared for the circumstances you may encounter. Right now, I would love to be working with Stacey on another case, but I need to give time to my new son, and my own family needs to take priority right now. Compromising our personal lives will not make us effective advocates for children.

Marsha

Steven has developmental and learning disabilities, as well as autism. During the years I worked with him, one of his strongest and most consistent interests was flags. Steven became concerned one day when we walked into a McDonald's and noticed that the United States flag, flying on the flagpole outside of the restaurant, was torn and seemed loosely attached to the flagpole.

"Look at the flag. It's torn. And it looks like it's going to blow away."

"Steven, you could tell the manager or cashier about the flag, and maybe he or she will make sure it's sewn or replaced," I suggested.

"I think I'll do that!"

Steven, who was usually shy and quiet when he ordered food, walked right up to the cashier and told her about the flag. She told him that she'd see what she could do.

The next week we drove by the restaurant. Much to my surprise, a new United States flag was waving in the breeze. Steven noticed it immediately.

"Look. It's a new flag!" he exclaimed excitedly.

"Steven, you made a difference!"

"The flag was changed because of me! The flag was changed because of me!"

Every time we drove by the restaurant, Steven noticed the new flag and was as excited as when he saw it flying for the first time.

The story I just shared deals with a case I worked on for seven years. I have been a CASA for nine years. During that time, I dealt with parents, a foster family, and the staff from the nonprofit agency that provided the school and housing for Steven. Although the usual CASA case concludes within eighteen months, and in fact, my other two cases closed within that time frame, Steven's case was much longer.

I was given the option to end my involvement with the case, as I had fulfilled my commitment. However, I stayed with it, because I was the only person with whom Steven interacted other than his school and group home staffs. He had virtually no contact with his parents and siblings, who lived out of state. Although this child had only a limited capacity to understand his situation, I do believe that it's important for every person to have someone in his life who's there for him and who isn't paid to be there.

I remember when I first read an article in the local paper about Advocates for Children. With my background in psychology and law, I figured being a CASA might be a good opportunity to combine the two while doing something that benefited children who needed help. As I continued in this work, I realized sometimes our involvement is more important than at other times. Regardless of the ultimate case development and resolution, with respect to every single case, the fact that an abandoned or neglected child has the full attention, support, and advocacy of one individual plays an important role for that child.

The court reports we write are an important contribution to the overall information provided to the judge or magistrate to enable him or her to make decisions with respect to the case. The magistrates I encountered were thorough and tried actively to obtain all relevant information to make the most informed and best decisions. I feel my contributions in court are mostly through my written reports and not through my verbal comments.

My experiences with the caseworkers and the guardians ad litem varied. Some of the caseworkers, in my experience, view the CASA as a necessary hindrance to dealing with their cases. I recognize that the caseworkers have a large number of active cases, which makes it difficult to give each case a large amount of attention. Generally, my experiences with the guardians ad litem were positive. In two of my three cases, they were active and engaged.

As a CASA, I worked with foster families in two of my three cases. In each case, the family was nice and receptive to my intervention. My cases were a bit unusual. In one case, the biological grandparents were the foster parents. In another, the foster family was designated through a private agency. Both foster families were consistently caring and loving toward the children, and both families were willing to answer my questions and discuss everything with me.

The only time I was worried for my safety was in regard to the father in one of my cases. Although small in stature, he was physically strong and made intimidating remarks to most of the individuals involved. In that particular case, I always kept my cell phone with me and advised my husband to be on notice if I didn't call by a certain time. Although I was concerned, I really didn't feel as if I was in danger because I felt that the individual's bark was much worse than his bite. I knew that he felt threatened by the legal system and that his reaction was to fight it in the only way he knew how.

For those considering this work, I have three pieces of advice: maintain a nonjudgmental open mind, maintain a sense of humor, and keep your goal of helping a child first and foremost in your mind.

Megan

For one of my cases, I had three little brothers, ages eight, five, and three. In my time as their CASA, I had been with them through three different foster homes. The oldest boy was like a dad to the others, always watching out for them, making sure they were feeling okay and had eaten enough. Whatever was happening, he was the protector.

For them, I felt that food was particulary a big issue. Every time I went to pick them up, their first questions were, "When do we get to eat something? Can we go to McDonald's?"

At the third foster home, I was to learn that it was going to be shut down. This was the first of several homes with which I would be involved that shut down for one reason or another. In this case, the father died and it was too much for the mother to continue fostering. I knew that, shortly, these three precious boys were going to be moved to foster care in a small town quite far away, and I'd no longer be their CASA. I was told that they had to be moved to this distant town because it was the only foster care home that could take all three brothers.

I knew that keeping the brothers together was important, especially since their biological mother no longer came to see them. At first, the oldest boy kept asking about his mother. After a few months, he stopped asking. The youngest boy continued to ask about his mother, but the big brother would tell him to stop asking because she wasn't coming. The oldest brother began asking me, "What's going to happen to us?" I tried to reassure him that all would be well in their new home.

Whenever I took the boys on outings, I'd take pictures of them. I wanted to make a little album for them to take with them to their new foster home. I worried, because the oldest boy would ask for a picture of me. I knew our relationship was growing, and I also knew it would be ending soon. I was trying to break the ties gently without breaking their hearts. When I gave them the album, the oldest boy started to cry. It almost broke my heart.

"Ms. Megan, this is really cool to see these pictures of us, but where is a picture of you?" he asked as he turned the pages of the book.

"I put a picture of me on the very last page, Ryan. Here it is."

I added my phone number and the date to the page as well, so the boys would always know they could reach me. After Ryan looked at my picture for a moment, he removed it from the back and put it on the front cover. At that point, I was almost in tears. Whenever I think of that moment, the tender feelings return. I did continue to stay in touch for about a year after they were moved. I would call and talk to the children. I would send them cards. At Christmas time, I would send them gifts.

As the example above shows, what I found hardest about being a CASA is the emotional ties that happen naturally and then must be broken when a case is over. These children who we help become like family, but then we must pull back as the case is winding down. It isn't easy to stop wondering how the children are doing and hoping that they're safe and happy. Understandably, after their cases close, many parents want to put their difficult custody struggles behind them and thus wish to cut ties with their children's CASAs. With most of my cases, I lost touch with the children after the court closed the case. In one instance, a grandmother got the children together about six or seven months later so I could see them. That was really nice.

I don't understand how I should feel as a CASA at times, because while I want to be close to the children, I know I must emotionally prepare for the time when the case is over.

Once I was the CASA for a teenage mom who had a one-year-old baby. She and I kept in touch for about a year after the case closed. She moved a lot, but she would always let me know where she was. When she was having a hard time, she would call for advice. I enjoyed helping her and bringing her and the baby gifts at Christmastime. After about a year, I never heard from her again. I asked my supervisor, "How can I know if she's all right?" The supervisor told me that if the young woman was ever involved in court again, the office would know right away — but in this work we hope to not have families returning to court, so, "no news could mean good news."

One thing I appreciated in doing this work is getting to know people from so many different backgrounds and cultures. I also appreciated learning new things through the ongoing trainings. I attend the book clubs, the films, and the workshops offering information on a variety of relevant topics.

I met some very helpful caseworkers. They kept me updated on what was happening from their end of things. At times, certain caseworkers would invite me to accompany them on visits to the children. It was always helpful to have that time to share insights on the case. Other caseworkers seemed too busy to have that two-way communication, and I had to beg to come along on visits or to share information.

I think that caseworkers have such a heavy workload that it's often hard for them to work with an additional person, such as a CASA. I remember one caseworker telling me she had twenty-five cases at the same time. That does seem like too many. The guardians ad litem, on the other hand, seem to find the time to keep in touch via email, and I'm usually able to work closely with them.

My biggest problem as a CASA, besides learning to emotionally disconnect when a case closes, has been working with the foster families. I had one particular case where the foster mother never called me back. She wouldn't pick up the phone, and even when I did reach her she wouldn't want to set up a visit. My visits were mandated by court, but she still refused to cooperate. When I finally got to her home, she opened the door, motioned me inside, and then sat on her couch. She never once made eye contact.

This was the way it was every time I went to visit my CASA teenager. At first, I thought it was due to my accent or the fact that I wasn't a white American. Then I thought that maybe she just needed to get to know me and that next time would be better, but the situation didn't improve. I continued to feel strange whenever I was in that home. It felt like the foster mother was trying to hide something. The end result of that particular situation was that the foster parent was doing a number of things that were unethical, and, in time, her home was shut down for foster care. From this experience, I learned to be suspicious of foster homes. I would go to foster homes with my eyes wide open until I knew it was a safe place for my CASA children.

In another case, a grandmother was given custody of her grandchildren. I didn't know that this woman had a history of mental instability. I was thankful that I was with the guardian ad litem on one particular visit, because after we were gone the grandmother called our CASA office. She said she wanted me removed from the case because I had arrived at her house drunk. She said she had smelled alcohol on my breath.

I couldn't believe it! I had no idea where this allegation was coming from or why this woman had such strong feelings against me. I called the guardian ad litem and told her what happened. She reassured me by saying, "Oh, don't worry. I was there. I know that's ridiculous. This woman is crazy. We have had to deal with her before. In fact, this woman made so many allegations against all of us that she had three different caseworkers and two different GALs already." Fortunately, this particular GAL and I were able to work on the case until it closed.

For those considering this volunteer work, I'd advise you that it might be hard to form attachments when you know in time you may lose contact with these children. However, don't let that stop you from having a chance to help a child have a better life.

Jerry and Leonora

Jerry: Sometimes you need patience for those little successes. It's been two and a half years since we were assigned to an especially complicated case.

Thirteen-year-old Ryan, ten-year-old Bob, and seven-year-old Jane were removed from their home and placed in foster care due to physical and alleged sexual abuse by their parents and possible sexual abuse by their siblings. Due to the concern of sexual abuse between the children, they each were placed in separate foster homes.

I was appointed to be Bob's CASA, while Leonora was given Jane, and the older brother was assigned to another CASA.

Bob has lived almost three years in his current foster care home, waiting for permanency in his life, while treatment plans and a termination of parental rights are ongoing. Bob adapted well to his foster home, but he misses his birth family in spite of his good foster care.

Jane, on the other hand, was shuffled between seven foster homes since her removal from her birth parents' home. Leonora has been with her through all these changes and has seen the negative impact the moves had on Jane.

Leonora and I spent many hours discussing our weekly

experiences with Bob and Jane. What was evident to us was the negative impact of the removal from their parents' home as well as the separation from their siblings. This was clearly showing up in the behavior of both Bob and Jane.

We realized quickly how important it was to the children to have a sense of belonging to someone, which they were gradually losing. Leonora and I brought up this subject to the caseworker and the guardian ad litem, as well as the court magistrate. Through persistence, we were granted the opportunity to allow Bob and Jane to have joint visits under our supervision. It was heartwarming to witness that first visit after Bob and Jane's long separation from each other. Our emotions were laid bare last Christmas when we were taking Bob and Jane to the CASA Christmas party. Before we entered the building, conversation between Bob and Jane got to the gut level. Jane was withdrawing, because she was asked about some recent bad behavior and she covered her face as if to hide.

"Please talk to me," Bob begged her. "You are all I have left in the world."

The emotions spread to Leonora and me, and it took us all more than fifteen minutes to regain our composure before joining the party.

Later in the year, serendipity rolled in. As a result of being told that her parents' parental rights were terminated, Jane's behavior in her foster home became unbearable. Her kinship foster parent, an aunt, gave up on Jane and told the Department of Human Services that they wanted her out of the house within a week. Due to the short notice, Jane needed temporary foster care. After many discussions and the support of Bob's foster mom, Jane was placed in the same foster home as Bob.

From then on, things have made an incredibly positive change in these kids' behavior and life. Leonora and I still visit with the children, and discussions with the children about adoption in a permanent home are ongoing. We are now confident that an adoptive home will be found for them in the not too distant future, giving them the love and permanency they deserve.

As a footnote, Ryan was reunited with his birth dad and seems to be doing well. We're working on having Bob and Jane reestablish contact with Ryan once some of the past negative issues are resolved.

Leonora began as a CASA about a year before I decided to join the work. I saw what a great way it was to help children, and I also figured it would be a good way to have a chance to talk to my wife. It has been great to be able to share a case, to talk about it with one another, and to bounce ideas off of each other.

Leonora: In the case Jerry mentioned, the children initially needed separate visits. We drove two separate cars. In time, the children were allowed to see one another, allowing us to take one car and to enjoy visits together with them.

Working with the legal people has its good points and its difficult points. We feel like the caseworkers and the guardians ad litem are doing their best. We realize they have many cases, and we have just one. We always share our information with them, but at times we get little feedback from them. We know that what we share is important for them to understand how the children are doing, so we just keep sending those emails. At times it's frustrating waiting for a response from the legal team, but during those times we just focus on the children. We're thankful that we, as volunteers, have the time to give to the children, to get to know them, and to serve them in the best way possible.

One thing I learned from this work is that there are a lot more cases of neglect and abuse and children suffering than I ever imagined. You only read in the paper about the biggest cases. Many children are under the radar, and even if they enter the legal system there aren't enough CASAs to help them all.

Jerry: To add to that, I would say that CASAs are essential to the well-being of children who are in the care of Social Services. It's essential to be an objective third party who can stand up in court and speak on behalf of the child. With the many cases that legal people have, we are the eyes and ears that they cannot always be. Rather than the law, our only concern is the children.

We were also impressed with the respect we find from the magistrate when it's time to go to court. We know that it's our responsibility to share our thoughts during the court hearing, and our particular magistrate makes that very easy. In fact, we know that she expects to hear from us, and we're called to the podium each time to share our thoughts on how the children are doing.

To anyone considering doing this work, I'd say that if you want to do this work, do it one hundred percent. This work is vital. The more you do it, the more you realize how critical it is. If you aren't willing to go the extra mile, it isn't going to work the way it should.

Leonora: I'd advise to get to know the children through conversation, through body language, through spending quality time together. You need to be available when the child really needs you. If you understand how they're feeling and where they're coming from, then you're able to better help them when they're feeling down or when they're in a crisis, such as when changing homes.

What Others Have To Say

You had a chance to read about our volunteers' experiences, including working with guardians ad litem, caseworkers, and their supervisors from the CASA office. Here are some comments from these professionals about their feelings toward the CASA volunteers.

Laura, Guardian Ad Litem

As a guardian ad litem who handles many dependency and neglect cases at one time, I very much appreciate having CASAs assigned to the cases. The CASAs are able to visit the children and the homes much more frequently. The observations and insights of the CASAs are invaluable to me in determining what is in the best interest of the children. On multiple occasions CASAs alerted me to situations that needed immediate attention to safeguard the children. I might not have determined they were significant issues upon which to take action for some time, since I do not have as frequent contact with the children. The CASAs I worked with are very dedicated to the children and their well-being. I appreciate all that CASAs do to make the difficult situations of being placed away from parents and being involved with multiple professionals and the court system easier and more enjoyable for the children.

YOLANDA BRYANT

Aimee Leifer, Legacy Project Coordinator, Former Caseworker

The one word to describe my previous job as an adolescent caseworker was hectic. When I originally took the job, I was told that I would work odd hours, travel a lot, and have an average of fourteen cases on my caseload. This didn't sound tough at the time. But, in reality, during a good week I worked fifty-five hours per week, traveled all over the state, on occasion traveled out of state, and had an average of eighteen cases, with some cases having as many as seven children.

As you can imagine, I quickly found out that there was never enough time in the day to complete my required face-to-face visits with all of the children while also building rapport, attending meetings, providing crisis intervention to the families, and completing all the necessary documentation. This is why I found CASAs were essential to my cases. As a previous CASA, I knew how important they could be to the child on the case by being supportive when the child felt like I, the caseworker, was just doing my job. As a caseworker, I enjoyed and wanted my CASAs to be involved as much as possible since I usually only saw the children once a month due to my hectic schedule.

I felt that CASAs had opportunities to build relationships with the children. I felt that they held unique insights into the families' or children's needs and truly could advocate for the children's best interests, whereas my role as the caseworker was very different. Sometimes I made decisions that I didn't want to make but that the department believed was the right thing to do. I know that CASAs are an essential piece to the children's success.

Unfortunately, as a caseworker, it was impossible to do my job as I felt it needed to be done, and I felt I could better serve children in another role. I am now the legacy project coordinator for Advocates for Children (a program within the CASA

106

organization that serves older teens that have been emancipated from the foster-care system). I truly believe CASAs have the opportunity to be the safe, supportive person for the children when they feel most vulnerable and alone. I truly believe in Advocates for Children's saying: "Be the difference, volunteer!"

Whitney: Adoptions Caseworker

I find the more recent CASAs to be very involved, often meeting weekly with the children. They provide opportunities for separated siblings to reunite through visits. Also, in a case of one child without siblings, the CASA provided an adult link that wasn't tied to the child's case. They met, did community outings such as grocery shopping, worked on craft projects together, took a dog for a walk, went to the post office, and did everyday things of this nature. This helped acclimate the child to the normal world around them.

The recent CASAs are sensitive to their role as a support for the children, rather than a support for the birth parents. They write thorough and well-stated court reports, which are useful and helpful. They attend LINKS (Listening to the Needs of Kids) meetings, school staffing meetings, and additional professional meetings. In general, they are truly helpful to the children on our cases.

Hillary, Guardian Ad Litem

One specific case comes to mind when I think about the work CASAs did to help me. I was the guardian ad litem appointed to a case involving two young children, a four-year-old and a six-year-old. Their father murdered their mother. The little boy even tried to stop his father, thereby actually witnessing the death of his mother.

An amazing CASA was appointed. It was my first time to work with Mary. To make a long story short, the Department of Human Services filed a petition; on the date it was to come to court, there was discussion of dismissing the case, as the parents of the mother had come forward and the courts were considering just giving the children to the grandparents. That didn't go over well, as no one knew anything about the grandparents. We agreed that these kids could go with their grandparents for the time being, but the case would stay open.

The CASA provided invaluable research prior to the two of us going out of state to investigate this family, as they all lived out of state. Mary tracked down all the family members on both sides of the family, and she created a family tree so I would know who was who. She interviewed all of the family members. When we arrived, she had appointments all set and knew who we needed to visit and where we needed to go.

In four days, we were able to assess that the grandparents weren't acceptable guardians for the children. We were able to find an aunt and uncle who would be a good support for the children. And, thankfully, those relatives were interested in adopting them. Without the help of Mary, we never would've known the best place for these children.

Throughout the years, I worked very closely with CASAs. They were always helpful to me. In fact, I am now a board member for the CASA organization. I am a big advocate for the work done by these volunteers.

Dani, Permanency Caseworker

I feel CASAs are helpful especially to younger children. They fill in the gaps between being with their parents, in foster care, around the caseworker, and visits by the guardian ad litem. I worked with a great CASA and a three-year-old. The CASA joined me on a couple of home visits, saw the child a few times each month, and also supervised a visit or two. Seeing me and the CASA together, having a visit with her mom and the CASA, and seeing the CASA outside of home visits and parent visits all were helpful to the child.

I believe this helped the child understand that many people were trying to assist her family. It allowed her to trust the adults in her life and made her feel important to many people. Overall, it helped her make connections because of the regular contact she had with her CASA throughout the case.

Wendy, Attorney and Former Guardian Ad Litem

I remember a particular case in working with a CASA that was extremely helpful. The young mother was missing, there was a warrant for her arrest, and her baby had been left with a relative. All attempts at finding this young lady had been futile.

The CASA assigned to this case did some research, found an old email address that this mother had used in the past, and decided to reach out to her in this way. She explained who she was, that she was not legally connected, nor paid to do this work, and that she visited her baby regularly. She then told her she would love to meet her for lunch somewhere, if she was interested.

The mother answered the email and the two of them met for lunch. The CASA was able to convince the young lady to turn herself in to the authorities. She promised to go with her to court. She also let her know how her baby was doing. Throughout the case the CASA kept a watchful eye on not only the baby, but the mother as well. When it began to look like termination of parental rights was going to happen, the CASA helped the young mother sort out her feelings and make the best decision for her baby.

CASAs have the opportunity to spend quality time with the children, as they only handle one case at a time. It is always beneficial to a child to have a number of concerned parties, such as the caseworker, the guardian ad litem, and the CASA. Three heads are always better than one. The CASAs I worked with have been conscientious, dedicated, and completely committed to the best interest of the child. The only problem with CASAs is that there aren't enough to go around.

Laura Hoffmann, CASA Supervisor

CASA volunteers often come to me a few months into a case and say to me, in a slightly embarrassed tone, that they don't feel like they're doing enough, that the kids on their case aren't doing well, and that it's hard to know how to help. This is extremely difficult for me as a coordinator, because I wish the volunteer could see themselves through my eyes.

What I want volunteers to know is that our role is well defined when there's a terrible problem that needs to be solved. When that child is bounced from home to home, it's very clear how to help as a CASA. When the child is failing in school, acting out during parenting time, engaging in self-harm, CASAs leap to fulfill the need, to figure out and to solve the problem. When something just doesn't feel right, and the volunteer can't put their finger on why, our volunteers get to the bottom of it and easily can point to those discoveries and subsequent solutions as work that they've done.

Our cases often go extremely well, like when the kids have relatives that want to raise them. Or when they are placed in foster homes that value the importance of maintaining family ties and want to provide those children with the best experiences and resources. Or when the biological parents get the message loud and clear and make drastic, lasting changes for the better. During those times, our role naturally becomes more in the background, as a positive, supportive adult who cares about the children. Honestly, this is the best outcome we can hope for. When those wonderful things are not possible or fall through, it's our CASAs who quickly find the work they need to do and fight hard for the children.

Tessa Holme, CASA Supervisor

I find that when I tell people what I do for work, most respond with some variation of the question, "How do you deal with reading about child abuse all day?" Most people then consider those of us who do this for our jobs as brave, one-of-a-kind types of people. However, supervising these amazing volunteers and seeing how involved and how in love with these children they become, I tell people that the volunteers are the brave, one-of-a-kind people.

During my year here, I've had the amazing opportunity to see these volunteers roll through the door, genuinely excited to begin their work in changing a child's life and being his or her voice. Of course, they're all seriously nervous to begin their first case, but what we as supervisors try to convey is that the children they will be spending time with are what we call them: children. These children indeed have suffered much trauma, but they are *not* their trauma. They are like every other kid on the playground, and they want to be treated like every other kid.

I can say that all my CASAs learn to view the kids on their cases as just another fun kid that they get to spend time with, to play with, and to give a voice to. To us supervisors and to our CASAs, these kids are not bad, they are not their trauma, and they are the same as your kid or mine. I love to watch my CASAs fall in love with their kids, grow passionate about them, and really fight for them. Seeing my volunteers do this raises my faith in humanity, especially in a job where it's so easy to lose that faith.

Kristin Kunz Martin, CASA Supervisor

After a case closes, the one thing I never tire of hearing is a CASA volunteer who says, "I think I got more out of this whole experience than the child did." I love hearing that sentiment expressed because I know this: The gift that these volunteers give when they commit their compassion, care, and voice to a child is greater than any gift these children likely have received in their entire lives. I also know that any person who is selfless, tenderhearted, and humble enough to say that they got the better end of that deal is a blessing to anyone lucky enough to cross paths with them. These are our CASA volunteers.

I'm blown away over and over again by the magnitude of

devotion that CASA volunteers have for the children. I know volunteers who drive a hundred miles one way, once a week, to let a lonely child know that someone cares about them. I know CASAs who shrug off cringe-worthy awkwardness, because a child needs a life lesson and has no one else to teach her. Time and again CASAs say to a child, "I'll be there," no matter the circumstances. Volunteers endure heartbreak so that they can see children live their hopes and dreams, and they rejoice in each child's successes. Most of all, every single CASA opens his or her heart to the children who otherwise might walk through life alone.

CASA volunteers light up the lives of those around them. At the end of a long day, I have the benefit of sitting back and smiling. Why? It's because, despite what volunteers might say about who's getting the most out of their experience, I know that I'm the one who makes out like a bandit, because I get to work with CASA volunteers!

Made in the USA
Coppell, TX
27 July 2020